ROCK
THE
PLANET ■ ■ ■

...Rock the Planet

Devotional readings from your favorite Christian entertainers ... compiled and edited by ■ *Steve Rabey*

Zondervan Publishing House
Grand Rapids, Michigan

ROCK THE PLANET
Copyright © 1989 by Steve Rabey

Published by the Zondervan Publishing House
1415 Lake Drive, S.E., Grand Rapids, Michigan 49506

Library of Congress Cataloging in Publication Data

Rock the planet : devotional readings from your favorite Christian
entertainers / compiled and edited by Steve Rabey.
    p. cm.
    ISBN 0-310-39781-2
    1. Meditations. I. Rabey, Steve.
BV4832.2.R612   1989
242–dc20   89–22566
                                                   CIP

All Scripture quotations, unless otherwise noted, are taken from
the HOLY BIBLE: NEW INTERNATIONAL VERSION (North
American Edition). Copyright © 1973, 1978, 1984, by the
International Bible Society. Used by permission of Zondervan Bible
Publishers.

Edited by David Lambert
Designed by Ann Cherryman

Printed in the United States of America

89 90 91 92 93 94 / AF / 10 9 8 7 6 5 4 3 2 1

■ contents

INTRODUCTION

The people in this book are used to standing before thousands of people. Whether they've become famous through concerts and recordings or through lectures, books, and articles, they have many followers. They're celebrities.

But for this book, I asked them to forget about that. Instead, I asked them to imagine themselves sitting in a church basement or school classroom with a dozen or so kids. I asked them to tell me what they would want to say to those kids.

I asked them to imagine one of the kids coming up to them to discuss some problem, maybe even a crisis. Many of these people didn't have to try too hard to imagine this—it happens to them often.

As these people told me their stories, they revealed much about themselves. They talked about their own struggles, their own insecurities, their own sins, the things in their lives that they would rather ignore or try to hide from God. And they told me how God loves us—no matter who or where we are.

I hope you enjoy reading their stories as much as I did gathering them. And I hope that you will be as touched as I was by these tales of honesty and hope.

HOW TO USE THIS BOOK

This book contains ninety stories or readings. If you read one a day, that will last you three months.

If you can, try reading one story every morning before you go to school or work. Or if evenings work better for you, read a story every night before bed.

But there's one thing to remember: This book isn't a substitute for Bible reading or prayer. Sure, these ninety stories can help you—but not as much as establishing a daily quiet time with God.

Maybe you can use these stories to help you do just that. If they mention a Scripture passage, look it up. Read it. Read the whole chapter. Read the next chapter, and the next.

You can also use these stories to guide your prayer. If you have struggled with the problems described in these stories, ask God to help. Or if he's already helped you, thank him.

The important thing is to begin inviting God into your life daily. If you do that, then God can really use you to *rock the planet!*

ROCK THE PLANET

Lost in the heavens
A blue crystal gem
In reckless spin
Wandering off course
Down from the heavens
Love came to be
And the world has seen no greater force

Hearts on fire
Rock the planet
We can make the world turn upside down
Cross that line
Rock the planet
Till the ground is shaking with the sound
It's time
Rock the planet
All we gotta do is take it to the heart
Inside
Rock the planet
And let the ways of Love be known

■ ■ ■

This revolution
Comes from within
And a change begins
With every choice
Set love in motion
Then watch it roll
Like long ago
Let's make some noise!

> *Hearts on fire*
> *Rock the planet*
> *We can make the world turn upside down*
> *Cross that line*
> *Rock the planet*
> *Till the ground is shaking with the sound*
> *It's time*
> *Rock the planet*
> *All we gotta do is take it to the heart*
> *Inside*
> *Rock the planet*
> *And let the ways of Love be known*

Words and music by Wayne Kirkpatrick, Chris Rodriguez, and Billy Sprague. © 1986 Tapadero Music (BMI) (a division of Merit Music Corp.), Skin Horse, Inc., and Edward-Grant, Inc. (ASCAP).

ROCK
THE
PLANET ■ ■ ■

We can rock the planet

■ *Billy Sprague*

What things—what world-changing people, ideas, movements, and inventions—have rocked our planet?

In the area of politics and war, you might list Alexander the Great and the Roman emperors. You'd also think of America's founding fathers, Napoleon, Abraham Lincoln, Hitler—and, of course, Doonesbury.

Inventions would include everything from the wheel, electricity, and nuclear power to pantyhose and jam boxes.

World-shaking ideas: "The world is round, not flat." Or, "All men are equal." Or maybe Einstein's theory of relativity.

But all of these people and ideas added together don't measure up to this one big idea: God became a man because he loved man so much.

God loves us so much that he died for us. What a mind-boggling idea! And here's another: Jesus is God. How about another one? Jesus rose from the dead.

No one else has rocked the world like that. We don't mark time year to year by the birth of any emperor, politician, writer, or inventor, no matter how powerful. We date all of history in relation to the birth of Jesus.

How did Jesus rock the planet? And how can we? Here's a simple but amazing answer: Love.

His power was love. Every heart that ever lived had spun off course because of sin. Jesus brought forgiveness, which mended people on the inside and put their lives back on course. And we can do the

same through the same power—the most powerful force the world has ever known—which is now ours (check Romans 5:5).

Look at Acts 17:6. What happened to the people who had been changed by Jesus' love? They began changing other lives—and even challenging the existing systems of thought and society. The angry mob called Christians "men who have turned the world upside down!" I like that.

I think *we* can rock our planet. But we have to remember three things.

1) Jesus said, "By this all men will know that you are my disciples, if you love one another" (John 13:35).

2) Jesus said, "You are the light of the world. A city set on a hill cannot be hidden ... In the same way, let your light shine before men, that they may see your good deeds and praise your Father in heaven" (Matthew 5:14-16).

3) And Jesus said, "Go therefore and rock the planet." Uh, that's my own version. What he really said was: "Therefore go and make disciples of all nations, baptizing them in the name of the Father and of the Son and of the Holy Spirit, and teaching them to obey everything I have commanded you. And surely I am with you always, to the very end of the age" (Matthew 28:19, 20).

Want to rock the planet? Then love someone—today. Let your light shine—today. Make a disciple—today.

Billy Sprague wrote "Rock the Planet" with Wayne Kirkpatrick and Chris Rodriguez. You can find it on Billy's "Serious Fun" album.

▪ ▪ ▪ We're Safe!

▪ *Morgan Cryar*

When I was in grade school in Louisiana, I played baseball. I was pretty bad.

I played any position where my coach thought nobody would hit the ball. At the plate, I probably got one hit my entire three years.

But once I got lucky. I walked, and then a teammate got a hit and I made it to second base on a close call.

But then the pitcher from the other side said, "Morgan, you're out!" I felt as if everybody in the whole park was looking at me. "You're holding up the game, Morgan," he said. "Go back to the dugout."

I believed him! I started walking back to the dugout—and then I saw my coach jumping up and down yelling, at me to get back on base. I dove—and just made it back as the pitcher tried to throw me out.

Years later, I realized that this story illustrates what our enemy does. Jesus died to forgive us. We have been called sons of God. But the Devil says: "Wait a minute—you're out! You've sinned. You're not good enough for God. Get out of the game."

And many times since then I've fallen for that same dirty trick, except that it wasn't a pitcher in a baseball game trying to fool me—it was Satan. But I *know* I'm safe now. All I need to do is stand confident where I am.

▪ *After he was unable to become a Major League baseball player, Morgan Cryar went on to become a popular Christian musician.*

Out of Control

Bryan Duncan

I was already exhausted from a bad weekend when I arrived in Dallas for a concert. The night before, I had gone to one city while my equipment went to another—which meant I had to play on unfamiliar keyboards. Worse, I had contracted laryngitis.

I was already frustrated—and that was before I stood waiting at the airport for a concert promoter who wasn't there. Obviously these people didn't think I was as important as I thought I was. As I stood at the ticket counter trying to get the next flight home, the promoter grabbed me.

I prayed hard for a miracle as I tried to adjust my attitude. Waiting quietly on God has never been an easy thing for me to do, but when I wait on him he makes the necessary adjustments to help me cope.

The concert that night in Dallas taught me that I can't always control everything that happens. It changed my whole approach to playing, and changed the way I see myself through God's eyes.

I grew that night. Because of my laryngitis, I invited members of the audience to join me on stage and lip-synch to tapes of my music! I smiled and laughed with them as they performed my entire set!.

What I learned that night is that God wants me more than he wants my talents. He even likes me—a lot. And the same is true for you.

■ *Christian artist Bryan Duncan is still searching for the perfect concert.*

We're all in this together

■ *Dana Key*

The members of our band are a mixed bunch, and we rarely agree on anything.

I'm nondenominational. Eddie is a Southern Baptist. Our drummer Greg is a General Conference Baptist. And Tommy, our bassist, is Pentecostal. We've all got different opinions on many subjects, and there have been a lot of lengthy discussions on our bus or in hotel rooms as we each try to convince the other that we're right!

To make matters more exciting, the four of us have traveled all over America, as well as parts of Europe and Africa. We've been in hundreds and hundreds of churches of different denominations—and some with no denomination at all. We've seen Christian believers do things and worship God in ways we would have never imagined possible.

Being raised in the Tennessee Bible Belt, I wasn't ready for what I saw. I had thought everybody pretty much believed and acted like the people I grew up with. But I realized that my little Christian world was small, and that God's family was much bigger and much more varied than I had expected.

I know that Christians disagree on many things: speaking in tongues and the gifts of the Spirit, the inspiration of the Bible, politics, and rock music, to name just a few.

But through reading my Bible and talking to Christians around the world, I've realized that all of us who follow Christ are part of one body, no matter what our social, cul-

■ ■ ■

tural, racial, or theological differences are.

In Matthew 16, Jesus asks Peter, "Who do people say the Son of Man is?" Simon Peter answered, "You are the Christ, the Son of the living God." Jesus replied, "You are Peter, and on this rock I will build my church, and the gates of Hades will not overcome it."

It's our commitment to Christ that unifies us—and if hell can't overcome that, then neither will our differences and arguments.

That doesn't mean Satan can't use our differences to hurt us. For instance, let me ask you something: Are the Christians at your school unified?

Or do they belong to different groups that don't talk to each other? Do the cheerleader Christians talk to the Chess Club Christians? Do the football-playing Christians pray with the Christians who play music? Do you and other Christians love the nerds and the unpopular people, or do you ignore them?

There's room for disagreements on all kinds of subjects. We can hold differing positions on tongues, music, clothing styles, and everything else. And we can be different and unique. God doesn't want us all to be carbon-copy, cookie-cutter people. But these things shouldn't separate us from each other.

There's one thing that's not open to debate, and that's our faith in Jesus and our need for his grace. That's what pulls us all together—if we let it.

■ *Dana Key is the lead guitarist and vocalist for DeGarmo & Key, a Christian band that began in 1972.*

How's your self-image?

■ *Margaret Becker*

Nobody's born perfect. That's OK. The problem comes when we begin focusing on our imperfections so much that we lose sight of even the good things about ourselves.

I struggled with this problem for about three years before I developed a way to confront my doubts and take them to God. It was a very simple plan: Whenever I had self-doubts, I would write down what I was feeling, and then I would trace those feelings back to their source. Then I would pray; I would take it all to God and lay it before him.

For instance: If I was feeling guilty about something, I would trace those feelings back to the wrong things that I had done. Then I'd write them down. My conclusion was that I was believing something that wasn't true about myself. After all, I had confessed my sins and mistakes, and God had forgiven me.

I believed other lies about myself: I'm not good enough, or I'm not pretty, or I don't know what I'm supposed to do, or nobody likes me. Some kids believe that their parents don't like them—or maybe they don't like themselves.

Once, I couldn't find a job, even though I looked for a long time. I traced that back to feelings that I wasn't good enough to get a job, or that I didn't have a skill, or that I didn't even know what I was doing with my life.

Then I looked up all the Bible verses on jobs, occupations, and skills. I read about how God used people's talents, or how he *gave* them

talents to fill an occupation or a calling he had for their lives.

I wrote those Scriptures down (believe me, my notebook got filled up pretty quick) to memorize for later on, because I knew the doubts would surface again.

When I doubted my worth, I memorized Psalm 139: "You created my inmost being; you knit me together in my mother's womb. I praise you because I am fearfully and wonderfully made."

When I compared myself unfavorably to other people, I would remember that God says that love is not envious, boastful, or proud (1 Corinthians 13:4),

When I felt proud, I would remember, "Pride goes before destruction, a haughty spirit before a fall" (Proverbs 16:18).

The Word of God is our sword against Satan's lies. And a sword doesn't do us any good unless we use it.

It's a way of holding up a mirror—God's mirror—to see ourselves by his standards. Then we can learn to see—and love—ourselves as he does.

Margaret Becker has recorded three albums for Sparrow Records.

25

DAY 6

■ ■ ■ Loving Indiscriminately

■ *Chris Davis*

Eight years ago I was walking down Main Street in my hometown of Mechanicsburg, Pennsylvania.

An older man was slumped over on the steps of a church. He hadn't shaved in a while, and he had a dirty checkered jacket on.

As I passed, he asked me if I could spare any money. I gave him enough for breakfast, and he said, "God bless you, brother."

At the time, I wondered whether I was being foolish. What was he going to do with the money? Buy wine? But then I realized that it wasn't up to me to decide how deserving a person in need was. I've been commanded by God to reach out to the people Jesus called "the least of these" (see Hebrews 13:2–3 and Matthew 25:34–40).

We shouldn't put ourselves in dangerous situations or let people make fools of us, but God tells us not to be discriminating about whom we show mercy and love to. We're instructed to help out.

Since then, I've wondered—could I have possibly been entertaining an angel, or even feeding the Lord himself?

■ *Chris Davis is a guitarist, singer, and songwriter for the band Glad.*

26

Don't Envy Sinners

Michael Peace

Sometimes it's tempting to look at sinners and all the fun they're having. But they don't have the promise of eternal life in Jesus Christ.

That's a problem for many Christian kids today—they want to do what their friends are doing, but their friends aren't walking with the Lord.

The Bible has a lot to say about how we should look at sinners, and it tells us clearly not to envy them (Proverbs 23:17 and 24:1 and 19). When it looks like sinners are having all the fun, remember that we've got something they don't—the promise of eternal life. Many of our friends will want what we've got if they see Jesus in us. And they will envy *us* if our lives reflect the power of God working in us.

That's not pride. Our lives are in God's hands. If the one who created the whole universe took the time to see that your life was touched and changed and affected by his power, then you've got all the reason in the world to be speaking up to your friends.

God is faithful to us even when we fail. If I fail I say, "Look, you've caught me on a bad day. But I am still forgiven of my weaknesses. When I am weak, Jesus is still going to be strong."

We all have our own personal weaknesses—but there's nothing anyone can do that will change who Jesus is.

■ *Christian rap artist Michael Peace doesn't envy anybody.*

27

God's secret agents

■ *Guy Doud*

As a schoolteacher, I see all kinds of kids in my classroom. Some belong to church youth groups. They don't always look differently or act differently; they don't have "church kid" tattooed across their foreheads. But they stand for something. I think of them as God's secret agents.

In one class, I asked, "What kinds of problems do you guys face today?" We listed them on the board. We had a whole range of problems, but the ones that seemed most widespread were getting along with the folks, drug and alcohol problems, loneliness, lack of self-esteem and self-worth, and feelings of inferiority.

So I asked the students to write about how just one of those problems had affected them.

One of the kids wrote about his family. All of his brothers had dropped out of school; all were alcoholics. His dad was an alcoholic. One of his brothers had been killed in a car accident. To make matters worse, at his brother's funeral, his dad had announced his decision to divorce the boy's mother.

It was an incredible essay. He went on: "Several weeks after the funeral, we got the doctor's report back from the examiner. And I found out that my brother had been drunk at the time of his accident. It was a head-on collision. The steering wheel pushed into his chest and pulled the big arteries from his heart by the roots."

Then he wrote, "It's too bad that something like that has to happen to make people real-

ize what they're doing to themselves and others. Maybe if people would take hold of something solid, like faith in Christ, maybe then and only then, will the troubles of our time be solved."

I'm a pastor of a church myself, but I can't preach a better sermon than that. It's the truth—we need to take hold of something solid. And Jesus is the solid rock. He's the foundation that lasts forever. He's the house that will never crumble. If we want permanency and something that will last forever, eternity, it's Jesus.

The student who wrote that essay had a lot of problems, but somehow, through all of his problems, he found something he could hold on to.

He found God, and he became one of God's secret agents.

The same can be true for us. In the midst of all of our problems, whether it be loneliness, fear, guilt, or lack of self-worth, we have to look to Christ.

He is the solid rock and the firm foundation. And if we build our lives on him, we have a foundation that will never crumble.

■ *Guy Doud, the 1986 National Teacher of the Year, has been hanging on to the solid rock since a junior-high teacher introduced him to Christ.*

29

Nerds run too
■ *James Ward*

OK, I'll admit it. In high school I wasn't a super athlete. I was never part of the "jock" scene. In fact, I once broke my finger playing softball in school, and in my senior year I hurt my back so bad that I needed to get an operation.

But still I appreciate the things Paul says about running the race and having the personal discipline we need to compete for the prize: "Do you not know that in a race all the runners run, but only one gets the prize? Run in such a way as to get the prize." Paul goes on to talk about the strict training the runner needs, and how Paul disciplined his body to make it his slave (1 Corinthians 9:24–27).

I appreciate this passage because I want to achieve something with my life, and that takes a lot of discipline.

But while we run, we need to ask ourselves what kind of prize we are seeking, and why it is we really want it. Jesus tells us there are two basic kinds of prizes: perishable and imperishable. The best prize is the imperishable, but sometimes it's hard to tell the difference.

Jesus said, "Be careful not to do your 'acts of righteousness' before men, to be seen by them. If you do, you will have no reward from your Father in heaven" (Matthew 6:1).

In the next verse he says, "When you give to the needy, do not announce it with trumpets." Those who do so "have received their reward in full." Instead, you should do your giving humbly, so "your

■ ■ ■

Father, who sees what is done in secret, will reward you" (Matthew 6:2–4). Next he tells us not to pray publicly to be seen by others (Matthew 6:5–8).

Is God saying he doesn't want us to pray or to help the needy? I don't think so. God just wants us to avoid false piety. If we serve others, we should do it privately and quietly. God promises to reward us.

We shouldn't try to fool ourselves. If we do things just to impress other people, they might think we're pretty neat Christian folks, all right. And although that might feel good, it's still just a perishable reward.

But if we do acts of righteousness for God, we will be rewarded with imperishable treasures that only God can give.

Try it—look around you for somebody who needs help or encouragement. Now go and meet this need without anybody else knowing about it. Or, instead of volunteering to give the prayer at your church, go home and pray alone for a while.

Get in the habit of doing good things for God, not for other people's applause and praise.

■ *While others were practicing football, James Ward was practicing piano. He now has nine albums to his credit.*

Lights on a hill

■ *Renee Garcia*

I was a Christian in high school, so I'm aware that sometimes a Christian is not the most popular thing to be. I also worked part-time at a dry cleaners, and I was the only Christian there.

Sometimes I was made fun of; some days I went home from school or work feeling rejected. Even though that hurt me, I believe that being known as a Christian in those situations was the most important thing I could do.

Jesus said to his disciples, "You are the light of the world. A city on a hill cannot be hidden. Neither do people light a lamp and put it under a bowl. Instead they put it on its stand, and it gives light to everyone in the house. In the same way, let your light shine before men, that they may see your good deeds and praise your Father in heaven" (Matthew 5:14–16).

There's more to being a Christian than getting saved and going to heaven. God wants us to reflect him while we are on earth—to let his light shine forth from us to others.

This is really the most important call on our lives: to live our faith daily. Everything we say, everything we do, can give light to people who are otherwise in the darkness—even if they mock us for it.

In our schools, where we work, going to the grocery, stopping at 7–11 to get a Coke, going to a football game, whatever else we do— what is the strongest testimony we can give? Just one simple thing—allowing Christ to be in us, and being so full of Christ and so sure of why we believe in him, that it overflows out of our lives.

What does that accomplish? It gives hope to people who are lost, because they realize that they can have God working in them, too.

When Jesus talked about being lights in the world, he wasn't talking to big-name celebrities. He was talking to his disciples, to normal people; he was talking about everyday circumstances.

He didn't say "You who sing on stage," or "You who preach sermons from the pulpit," or "You who are on television," or "You who run things and own things." This Scripture is meant for everybody, in any circumstance, on any day.

I know it can be tough. I didn't like being made fun of for my faith. But you know what I found out? A lot of people who were poking fun at me would, in times of crisis, come to me for help.

One said, "I have this really bad problem and I need help. I know you're not just a follower—you've stuck to what you believed, so I know you won't let me down. Can you help me out?"

Handling ridicule isn't easy, but sticking to your faith is worth the sacrifices. That's the only way we can be lights in this dark world.

After singing and touring with Amy Grant, Renee Garcia released her debut album in 1987.

■■■ Who Are You?

■ *Bobby Michaels*

A few years ago, if someone asked me who I was I would say, "I'm Bobby Michaels, the Christian singer."

That was the answer I gave once in a class with one hundred other Christians—but someone asked me, "Who are you *really*? If someone took away your voice who would you be? Are you afraid that people—and maybe God—can't like you just for you?"

For the rest of our time together, I had to relate to people as me, not as "a recording artist." It was like drug withdrawal. But I learned that we all hide behind the "identities" we create in our jobs, or our sport, or our special skill (like music).

I met a high school student who had been his school's best athlete before he lost his legs in a car wreck. He had to adjust to never *walking* again,

let alone running. He told me, "My whole identity was wrapped up in running. Now I realize that my identity needs to be wrapped up in Christ. That's the only thing that won't change."

My self-image had become an idol. I was serving my idea of who I was instead of God.

Who are you? After you strip away titles like "cheerleader," "musician," "good student," "church member," and others, what is left? Begin finding your identity in Christ, your Lord.

■ *Bobby Michaels is a servant of Christ who just happens to sing.*

We Can't Stand Too Tall

Rick Cua

On my new record, there's a song called, "Can't Stand too Tall." The words go:

"I've got to dig my feet in and listen when He calls / You can't stand too tall when you cross that river / Gonna face it all on your way to the other side / You can't stand too tall or too close together / We won't fall cause He'll keep our heads above the water / You can't stand too tall."

We can never stand *too* tall for Christ—we've got to go for more. We can't be complacent. We shouldn't be happy to just break even.

Some people are content to sin and then repent, sin and repent, over and over. That's only breaking even. Forget that! Let's charge ahead for the Lord.

Breaking even is no way to live. It's mediocrity. It's lukewarm and wimpy. In everything we do—not just worship and prayer and witnessing, but in our lives, our homes, and our jobs—we've got to stand tall. Anything we take on, we've got to do with that kind of zeal. That's a fruitful life. And that's the way God wants us to live.

Things aren't always going to be easy—but we can win if we stand tall for God and give our all to everything we do.

 Rick Cua, former bass player for the band Outlaws, is a popular Christian artist.

Finding your place in the puzzle

■ *Mike Warnke*

Imagine this: you're assembling a jigsaw puzzle with nine thousand pieces. You choose the puzzle because it's attractive and it looks like fun. You spend good money for it. You clear off the table, and you spend hours and days carefully assembling it piece by piece.

Then, when you're just about finished, you realize you're one piece short. The beautiful picture that you worked so hard on is not complete. There's a hole in your picture, and that's no good.

That's how God sometimes feels about us. After all, life is like a big jigsaw puzzle that God is putting together. But without every piece, the picture will be incomplete. And why shouldn't he have every piece? He bought us with a price (the

death of his son), and he works hard to assemble us into his body. But we gripe and grumble and argue with God. The problem is that often we want to be a different piece than God made us. We look around at the rest of the puzzle and decide we want to be a piece of the clouds, or a piece of the windmill, or a piece of the flowers.

But without the pieces of grass and the pieces of earth and the pieces of bridge—the picture is never complete.

When we act that way we not only hurt ourselves, but we also hurt the other pieces of the puzzle who depend on us. Because each of the pieces fits together with its neighboring pieces. Each piece stays in place because the neighboring pieces support it.

That's important too—the support we all get from others.

You know, even celebrity-type people like me sometimes wish we were another piece of the puzzle.

There are times when a comic wishes he were a musician, and a musician wishes he were a writer, and a writer wishes he were an entertainer, and an entertainer wishes he were a pastor, and a pastor wishes he were a missionary, and a missionary wishes he were an evangelist, and an evangelist wishes he were a pastor!

It happens to everybody, regardless of who you are or what you've got. There will be times when somebody else's situation looks a whole lot better.

But we need to learn to be content with what God made us and where he put us. The place that God puts you is where you'll be most effective.

Of course, we can try to do something different—to be another piece of the puzzle. But what happens on your jigsaw when you put a piece in the wrong spot? Not only does the picture look funny, but you usually get your corners bent out of shape and you wind up looking ridiculous.

In a puzzle, pieces of flowers don't belong in the sky. The sky doesn't belong over on the bridge, and the bridge doesn't belong on the windmill.

Likewise, you don't need to try to be somebody else somewhere else doing something else. God didn't ask you to give away other people's talents—he only asks you to give what you have—yourself!

 Comic Mike Warnke is happy being comic Mike Warnke.

■ ■ ■ God's Pipeline

■ *Randy Stonehill*

Jesus was speaking to a crowd of more than 5,000 people.

As the day wore on, his disciples said, "Hey, let's send the crowds away to the villages so they can buy some food for themselves."

But Jesus said, "Don't send them away—give them something to eat" (Matthew 14:16). So the disciples gathered up five loaves of bread and two fish and they fed the whole crowd. And when they gathered up the leftovers, they wound up with more than they'd started with.

What a powerful, simple story! I used to think of it as something Jesus did to show his authority, but now I see it as Christ's way of saying, "If you are open-hearted in giving what you have, won't I be faithful to give you more?"

I've seen this firsthand in the work of Compassion International, when people give a little in faith. If we will look at the hurting, the hungry, and the needy, we can't help but hear Jesus telling us today: "Don't send them away—reach out and help them."

God is our source. All we need is to be willing to be a pipeline for his love and truth and power, and our lives will be full.

■ *Randy Stonehill has been active in moving people to do something about the needs of the poor and hungry of this world.*

Not of This World

Robin Crow

I perform most of my music at colleges, which gives me a great chance to see how Christians relate to the world.

Often I see fifteen Christians standing off in the corner. They form their own little closed Christian culture club. Sometimes they talk to me after a concert, using so much Christian lingo that *I* can barely figure out what they're saying. I wonder how non-Christians can understand them.

Then there are people like Rolf, who was the student activities director at St. Johns University in Minnesota. Here was a guy who was just as hip and as involved in campus activities as anyone there; he was also a deeply committed Christian who was studying to be a pastor.

I didn't even know he was a Christian until I told him how much I admired him. He was a really great guy and he handled his handicap very well (he had no legs). That's when he told me about his faith.

He didn't preach or wear Christian bumper stickers on his wheelchair. He simply displayed Christian virtues—and he did it out in the middle of things, not on the sidelines.

Rolf showed me we can fit into school or college and be a Christian at the same time. He was, simply, what Christ asked us to be: in the world, but not of it. Thanks, Rolf.

Robin Crow takes his guitar to hundreds of colleges every year.

God is our hiding place

■ *Steven Curtis Chapman*

I was invited to do a concert at a church in Texas, and when I got there the youth pastor said, "I want to share with you how we heard about you and why you've been asked to play here tonight."

He told me about a girl who had come to see him about a year before, in tears.

She was pregnant. "I found out a couple of days ago," she said. "The father of the baby is giving me money for an abortion. I'm gonna go that route—I just can't take the pressure. My father doesn't care about me; he hasn't even talked to me in five years. So I'm gonna have to deal with this alone."

She left—but she came back a week later. She had not yet had the abortion; she wanted to do something to make things right. She knew she was suffering the consequences of her sin, but she was a Christian, and she knew she was forgiven.

The church found her a home for unwed mothers. Everything was going OK, but a few months later all the shame and guilt came down on her like a ton of bricks. She realized that, soon, she would have to go back and face her family and friends, who would scorn her.

That night, one of her girlfriends gave her a tape with my song "Hiding Place" on it. She listened—and heard that God's grace is her hiding place in the storms of life.

Jerry Salley and I, who cowrote the song, based it on Psalm 32:6–7: "Therefore let everyone who is godly pray to

40

■ ■ ■

you while you may be found; surely when the mighty waters rise they will not reach him. You are my hiding place; you will protect me from trouble and surround me with songs of deliverance."

In the song, Jerry and I wrote, "I'm not asking you to take away my troubles Lord, 'cause it's through the stormy weather I learn to trust you more. You're unfailing love surrounds me when I need it most 'cause you're my hiding place."

She realized that God didn't want to punish her or ignore her or condemn her—he just wanted to love her. God wouldn't lift her completely out of this situation and take her into another realm. Instead, he was saying to her, "Let me put my arms around you. I want to pick you up and carry you through this. You'll still have to face the consequences of this— as well as your family and friends. But remember, I'm your hiding place. Allow me to love you and give you the strength to face this."

I met that girl that night after my concert. She was one of the leaders of their youth group. She was beautiful. Sixteen years old, and full of energy. Her whole outlook had changed after she listened to "Hiding Place," and God began to teach her that he wanted to surround her with love and deliverance and to comfort her.

■ *The song "Hiding Place" is from Steven Curtis Chapman's first album, "First Hand."*

41

Maturity, one day at a time

■ *Mike Atkinson*

Being mature. That was my goal as a teenager. In fact, many teenagers want the respect that comes with being mature.

"I'm getting older—it's time to be taken seriously," I would say to myself when I was thirteen.

But what usually happened was that, instead of acting maturely, I was just trying to "act like an adult." That meant everything from driving a car before I was old enough, to staying up late to smoke and drink. Those things didn't make me an adult, let alone mature.

Sometimes when I read my Bible I'm miles away mentally. But one morning the word *mature* caught my eye: "All of us who have grown spiritually to be mature should think this way, too" (Philippians 3:15, NIV). I

thought to myself, "Think what way? How do mature people think?" That led me back to the previous paragraph, which I had missed earlier:

"I do not mean that I am already as God wants me to be. I have not yet reached that goal. But I continue trying to reach it and to make it mine. Christ wants me to do that. That is the reason Christ made me His. Brothers, I know that I have not yet reached that goal. But there is one thing I always do: I forget the things that are past. I try as hard as I can to reach the goal that is before me. I keep trying to reach the goal and get the prize. That prize is mine because God called me through Christ to the life above" (Philippians 3:12–14, NIV).

Paul was saying that maturity takes time and requires humility. He's saying: *I haven't obtained it; I'm not perfect; I have not arrived.*

I understand that God's ways are not man's ways. God tells us to do things like love the poor, not the rich; give up our lives, not save them; turn our cheek; don't fight back. These things don't come naturally to me.

Maturity is like that too. It's not natural for us to be mature and humble. Most adults *think* they're mature and humble. Just ask them! But I wonder if they really are.

Once again, God shows how radically different his wisdom is from the world's. To be mature means to realize and accept that you are not yet who God wants you to be, and that you have a lot of growing ahead.

What made Paul humble was his desire to move toward the goal of God's best for him, and his constant effort to get there. That's ambition—but not ambition driven by pride. Instead, it's driven by some tough, humbling realizations.

God wants us to be honest with ourselves and with him about our relationship to him, our shortcomings and weaknesses. Developing that spiritual talent will put you squarely on the road to maturity.

Mike Atkinson is editor of "Media Update," a publication of Menconi Ministries. He is also a columnist in "The CCM Update."

43

... God Wants Us

Fred J. Heumann

A guy named James Weldon Johnson wrote a poem called "The Creation" in which God says, "I'm lonely. I'll make me a world."

I thought, *See, that proves God needed me.* I used to tell people God made man because God needed a family—someone to share his love with.

I took this personally, too. I thought God needed my ministry because nobody else was doing what I was doing—until somebody pointed out that the God of the Bible has no needs.

I began to see that I can't do anything that will make him more God or less God. He is the same yesterday, today, and forever. Plus, God didn't need me to love. In the Trinity, there was already perfect, eternal love between the Father, the Son, and the Spirit.

At first, that upset me—God didn't need us! But then I realized something great: he wanted me. He wanted you. And he loves us all.

The Bible tells us that God chose us before the foundation of the world (Ephesians 1:4). It also tells us, "You did not choose me, I chose you" (John 15:16). He chose me because he wanted me.

I was living by a false value system, thinking I could do something for God to earn his favor. But I was wrong. He wanted me already.

Fred J. Heumann doesn't believe God "needs" him, but Fred still serves God as Director of Music Ministries for YFC International.

Who Is Your Gatekeeper?

Ken Davis

Ghengis Khan was a famous warrior who stormed across China conquering, sometimes without bloodshed, cities that were fortified by huge, thick walls. When someone asked him how he managed to gain entrance to these protected cities, he smiled and said: "We bribed the gatekeeper."

Most kids today don't even *have* a gatekeeper—not a mental one, anyway. As a result, they let every thought, every picture or movie, every song, every fantasy into their minds. They've never made the decision to say, "I will not let this thing into my mind."

The Bible tells us to bring every thought captive to Christ, and part of giving God our lives and minds is deciding that we are going to put a gatekeeper over our minds.

It helps to keep our minds saturated with the Word of God. God's Word tells us what's good, bad, and ugly. It tells us what's right, wrong, and out of the question. And by feeding our brains with the Bible, we'll be better able to fight against invading thoughts and images that don't belong there.

It's impossible for us to truly follow God and do his will if we haven't surrendered our minds to him. But when God has our minds, our bodies, and our wills, he has pretty much all of us, and we can trust him to guide us and direct us in our lives.

■ *Writer and speaker Ken Davis surrendered his mind to God years ago, but it still works pretty well.*

Tools for God

■ *Dana Key*

My phone number used to be listed in the Memphis phone book. That was before the arrival of the "Crazed Caller."

I didn't know his name, his age, or where he lived—but I did know four things about him: he seemed somewhat mentally unbalanced; he was a big fan of DeGarmo & Key; he thought I could help him; and he would do anything he could to talk to me on the phone.

On a typical day, he would call three or four times—at all hours of the day and night.

I cared about this mysterious caller, and I prayed for him often. But he was calling me so often that I had to come up with a solution. I told all my friends, "Look, this guy is driving me crazy. If you want to call me on the phone, let my

phone ring once, hang up, and call me back."

That helped—but one big problem remained. Some nights when my family was sound asleep, he would call three or four times and let the phone ring over and over.

So I tried unplugging the phone—but that meant I couldn't receive calls from people I needed to talk to.

Finally, I broke down and got an unlisted phone number. And my problem with the Crazed Caller was over.

But you know what? Never during all of these problems did I think that the problem was really with the phone itself. I knew the problem was with the Crazed Caller, who was abusing and misusing the phone.

God is the creator of everything. Satan, in his rebel-

■ ■ ■

lion, has perverted many areas of God's perfect creation, but he has no power to bring into being things that did not previously exist. He can only rearrange, taint, or pervert that which God has already created.

And that is just what he has done in many areas of communication and art today: music, television, books, and radio. But the good news is that these areas are God's first. And if Satan has temporarily claimed them, we can reclaim them and return them to the service of the Creator. That's why my partner Eddie DeGarmo and I use rock and roll—which has often been used to communicate an ungodly message—as a tool to convey the healing, saving message of Christ.

The important thing to remember is that it's up to us to use the tools God has given us. We can use the telephone to bring good cheer or to make obscene phone calls. We can use music to bless or condemn. And we can use our eyes, ears, and mind to take in things that are bad or things that are good. It's up to us.

And don't forget: Your life is a "tool" too. God has given you that life along with many talents and gifts, and you can use these gifts to serve God and man or you can use them to hurt.

It's up to you.

■ *This discussion was taken from Dana's brand new book on Christian music,* Don't Stop the Music *(Zondervan, 1989).*

47

... Having Fun?

■ Ed DeGarmo

"I don't want to become a Christian now. I'm young. I want to have some fun!"

I used to think like that. My plan was to do whatever I *wanted* to do—get rich, travel around the world, maybe have a family, and enjoy life. Then, when I turned 50 or 60 and death was on its way, I would begin to get serious about God.

It should be just the opposite. God wants us to serve him in our youth.

Serving God while you're young isn't a popular idea in America. We're bombarded with advertising about having fun while we can, as if when you turn 30 you shrivel up! All the companies who advertise beer, cars, and clothes tell us to think about today and forget about tomorrow.

Solomon would have liked today's ads. He wanted to have fun when he was young. But when he got a little older he was pretty burnt out. "Everything is meaningless," he said. And in Ecclesiastes 12 he tells us, "Remember your Creator in the days of your youth."

But you've been living only for yourself for 50 or 60 years, it's hard to say, "OK, today I'm going to begin serving God." Begin serving God today. It's not always easy, but it's the most exciting thing you can do!

■ *Ed DeGarmo of the band DeGarmo and Key isn't a teenager anymore, but he is still having fun serving the Lord.*

Lonely Prayer

Solveig Leithaug

Agirl I went to school with was afraid to talk to me, so she wrote me notes. One note said, "I am lonely. I can only talk to God and my cat." I wrote my song "Lonely Prayer" about this girl.

I get lonely myself. I travel so much that I can't be with any of my friends. When I am home, they have things to do and can't drop everything for me. Here are some things that help me with my loneliness:

First, I have learned to be a friend with myself. Some people don't like themselves, but I'm becoming better friends with myself everyday!

Also, books and movies help. A good novel can take me far away. My favorite is *Christy* by Catherine Marshall, but there are many others.

When the pain of loneliness seems unbearable, another thing that helps me is to cry! It helps wash out the pain I am feeling. Crying isn't just for girls—God gave boys tear ducts too!

I also try to develop strong friendships. I can count my true friends on one hand. Friendship is hard work, and it requires an investment of time—we don't have time for more than a few friends.

Finally, I know that God is always with me. I don't hear his voice like some people do, but I know he is in my heart leading my life.

■ *Solveig Leithaug travels throughout Europe to sing her songs.*

In it for the long haul
Pete Carlson

One of the most difficult things for me to deal with in my life is to realize that we are in this erratic life for the long haul.

So often I'm inclined to run to the Lord for the quick fix, to have him slap a band-aid over the problems in my life. I figure that if he can just get me through today, everything will be wonderful.

But God doesn't work on the quick fix. He doesn't tell us that if we follow three easy steps, everything will be wonderful by lunch time.

One of my biggest challenges is being able to put my life into a long-term eternal perspective. We all need to realize God is a God of *process*. He's working on us bit by bit, and we can't rush him.

When we get buried by the circumstances of our lives and just can't seem to clear the air, we go to seminars, workshops, retreats, Christian concerts, speeches, youth meetings, and church to search for a quick answer—or at least for an emotional charge that will make us feel good for a moment.

And in our search to feel good again, we never really deal with some of the big messy problems beneath the surface.

If we're going to really grow, we need to dig beneath the surface of our lives and not just gloss over things. That can be very painful—but life is often painful. We just have to accept that.

Life isn't a merry-go-round. It's going to stretch us in different directions—maybe in direc-

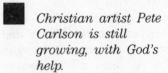

■ ■ ■

tions we've never expected or planned on.

Some of the problems we have in our lives are complex, and it takes time to sort them out. We can't just read a few Bible verses and think everything's solved.

Yes, God has given us his Word to communicate truth to us; yes, he wants us to seek out his Word at times of depression, chaos, and confusion. But the process of working the bugs out of our lives can be slow. As we put our eyes on Christ and dig into his Word, the process slowly begins to reveal itself to us.

Remember this: God is not the God of a quick fix; instead, he works through process. If it's painful for a while, relax— the overall result is growth. The struggle is always going to be there, but God is always with us through that struggle.

■ *Christian artist Pete Carlson is still growing, with God's help.*

Watching the champs

■ Phil Madeira

When I was a kid, my dad took my best friend Wayne and me to see the Boston Red Sox play the New York Yankees at Fenway Park.

In those days, any normal, red-blooded American kid automatically loved the Yankees. They had Mickey Mantle and other great players. Those were the big years of Yankeedom.

It was a fun day. Wayne and I loved the belligerent fans, the hot dogs, the snacks, and running all around the stadium. I can't even remember who won the game, we were having so much fun.

What I do remember, though, is that I had a pair of white deck pants. They were like jams, except they came down to my knees. And they had a rope for a belt. In retro-spect I have to admit they looked pretty stupid. But back then everyone was wearing them.

As the afternoon wore on, my snazzy white pants were getting filthier and filthier. By the time Wayne and I got back to our seats they weren't very white anymore.

My dad looked at me and said, "Philip, how did you get so dirty?"

My answer was really pretty profound. I said, "Well, I guess it's a pretty dirty place."

Twenty years later, I think that's a pretty good illustration of what being a Christian is like.

As Christians, we have been cleansed by Christ. All our sins have been forgiven. If we're walking with Christ, our old habits, old sins, and even our old ways of thinking have been changed and cleaned up.

But the world we live in is a dirty place. Even though God has cleaned us up, it's easy for us to get dirty and tainted—by things we see on TV, by songs on the radio, or by things the people we hang around with at school say.

I still go to Yankee Stadium to see the Yanks—-about once a year, with my wife Elinor and my Dad and brother. These days the *game* is more interesting to me than what's happening in the stands or the concessions area.

None of us wants to miss an inning or even a play. The coke and hot dog vendors come around sooner or later, so we can devote our attention to the champs.

It brings to mind something Saint Paul once said: "When I was a child, I talked like a child, I thought like a child" (1 Cor. 13:11).

The world offers us excitement and things good and bad to divert our attention from the real game of life. Jesus wants to be the center of our lives, and when we take our eyes off him, it's hard to keep the dirt of sin off ourselves.

He asks us, "How did you *get* so dirty?" He doesn't ask out of meanness or ignorance— he already knows where we've been and what we've done.

When we come to him, dirt on our deck pants, he will, like a loving Dad, gently forgive us. He'll wash us up—and he'll never deny us a good seat for the big game, right next to him.

Long ago, Phil Madeira gave up on playing professional baseball to devote himself to a long and fruitful career of making music.

DAY 25

■ ■ ■ What Feets!

■ Duffy Robbins

Think about your feet for a minute. What comes to mind? Maybe they get sore sometimes. Maybe they smell funny all the time. But your feet are very important.

Your feet help you walk 115,000 miles every year. That's equal to walking across North America 35 times.

Also, feet are important in medical research. The Harvard School of Public Health once collected 50,000 sets of toenail clippings to try to find the cause and cure of cancer.

Your feet are important to God too. He talks about feet all through the Bible: "Make level paths for your feet" (Hebrews 12:13). "Stand firm . . . with your feet fitted with the readiness that comes from the gospel of peace" (Ephesians 6:14–15). And, "How beautiful are the feet of those who bring good news" (Isaiah 52:7).

Why does God talk about our feet so much? Because our feet help us make a stand— where our feet are planted, that's where we are. But more importantly, our feet tell God which direction our lives are going, and where we're going to be tomorrow, next year, and for the rest of our lives.

God cares about our feet, and he's concerned about our direction in life. Where are your feet taking you?

■ *Footnote on Duffy Robbins: His feet continually carry him to talk with young people and youthworkers.*

Who Does God Love?

Roger Judd

Roger Judd is a graphic artist and free-lance cartoonist living in Upland, Indiana, with his wife and daughter.

God can take a joke

■ *Randy Thomas*

I see two extremes in how Christians live out their faith. Some are too laid back and liberal, and think God is the nice big guy up in the sky. Others are uptight and legalistic, and they think God is the cosmic policeman who wants to slap our hands and spoil all our fun.

One thing that helps me find a balance between those extremes is realizing that God is not only somebody to be reverenced and served and loved as an omnipotent Creator, but that he also has a sense of humor.

Now I know that some Christians say, "We shouldn't be joking, should we?" But I believe God created humor along with everything else. He can tell whether we're joking.

There's a story in 1 Samuel, chapters 5 and 6, that proves to me beyond a shadow of a doubt that God has a great sense of humor.

The Israelites lost the ark of the Lord to the Philistines in battle, and the Philistines put the ark in the temple of their god Dagon. The next morning, when they went into the temple, Dagon had fallen on his face before the ark of the Lord—as if he were worshiping.

The Philistines stood Dagon back up and went about their business.

The next morning when they came back to the temple, not only had Dagon again fallen before the ark of the Lord, but parts of old Dagon had broken off. The Philistines still didn't get the idea.

But soon afterward, they began to wonder. God inflicted them with "tumors of the groin," or hemorrhoids (if you don't know what they are, ask your parents). I'm sure that wasn't funny to them, but to me this is God playing a great joke on these disobedient people—even being mischievous.

Next, those smart Philistines took the ark to another area of their country, and *those* people got hemorrhoids. Then they sent it to a third place—bingo: hemorrhoids. This went on for seven months, and this was long before the day of Preparation H!

Finally, the Philistines woke up and decided to give the ark back to Israel, but before they did so they crafted some gifts to the God of Israel: five golden mice and *five golden hemorrhoids!* They put all this stuff on a cart pulled by oxen and said, *If the God of Israel is the Lord, these oxen will find their way back to Israel.* And sure enough, the oxen took the ark straight back to Israel.

When these folks captured the ark, they thought they were pretty neat. They said: "We've captured the Lord. This proves we're the greatest!"

They had a haughty spirit. God had about enough of that and began handing out hemorrhoids, showing that, even when he's correcting us, he has a sense of humor.

Randy Thomas, who was a founding member of Sweet Comfort Band, now plays guitar with Allies.

57

Fighting slogans with the word

■ Michael Peace

When you aren't committed to the Word of God, all kinds of things can slip into your head. I'm finding a lot of kids grabbing onto slogans or sayings that aren't really doing them any good.

I see kids accepting slogans like "safe sex," when the only kind of sex God calls safe and good is between married people.

How about "just say no"? There are things we should say no to. But there are so many times God wants us to say yes.

When the kids at my church tell me the slogans and sayings that are going around, I tell them to fight back with slogans of their own.

One thing I say is, "The next time you get peer pressure, put the pressure on." What I mean by that is when a person tries to push drugs or sex or alcohol on you, you push the Lord on them. Just tell your friends, "Every time you come my way with drugs and alcohol, I'm going to tell you about the Lord Jesus Christ." You're putting the pressure on. That's the kind of peer pressure that's going to affect people's lives.

Don't sell out to cowardliness. Don't sell out to foolishness. Don't sell out to lies. Don't sell out what you believe in.

A lot of kids say, "Well, that sounds real good, but how do I take this back to my neighborhood?"

Anybody who was ever totally committed to what they believed in, who took risks to bring about change, had the attitude of a revolutionary.

Just look at Jesus. He

was always getting people mad by upsetting their apple carts. Remember the time in the temple when he overturned the tables of the moneychangers and the people who were selling things in God's house?

And he was always fighting against sin, sickness, and death. That's why he forgave people their sins, healed them from their illnesses, and brought them back from the dead.

He was a true revolutionary—and you can be a revolutionary too, if you follow God's commands. If you have that kind of commitment you will be confident of where you're going in life.

Here's a slogan for you: If you aim at nothing, you're going to hit nothing. If your head and heart are empty, emptiness will come out of you.

The Bible says that out of the abundance of the heart, a man speaks. So, out of the abundance of your heart, you should be speaking those things that are true. You should be bearing fruit from your love for God and your time in his Word.

If you want people to take you seriously, you've got to be serious about being taken. And the best way to be serious is to stand on God's Word. It's faithful and true, and can guide you in all areas of life.

 Michael Peace is a College and Career pastor and assistant to the youth pastor at Bethel Full Gospel Church in Rochester, New York.

DAY 29

■ ■ ■ Paradoxes

■ *Rich Mullins*

Life is a paradox (that means something that seems to contradict itself).

Look at God and man: God has sovereignty and we have free will. God is sinless but we, his creation, are sinful. It's confusing!

The Bible character Job dealt with plenty of paradoxes. He was just minding his own business when suddenly a lot of terrible things happened to him. He said, "God, what in the world is going on?"

When God heard Job's cry, he didn't give Job an answer. God just showed himself to Job. And once Job saw the Almighty, he didn't need an answer anymore. He even forgot about the question.

Life is like that sometimes. Things happen to us that we don't understand. Our nice plans get all bent out of shape.

If we turn to God like Job did, God will help us make the best of our current situation. That doesn't mean he'll make everything perfect, or that he'll answer all of our questions. But he will strengthen us.

But if we try to make God make sense, it won't work. We'll never get to know God that way—he's just too big! We can't see all the sides of him, and we can't understand everything that happens. But when we seek God, and when God gives us himself, everything will work out just fine.

■ *Christian artist Rich Mullins doesn't know everything, and he doesn't even try. But that's OK. He's understanding God more and more.*

YMISIM?

Billy Sprague

I heard a preacher say once, "There's a dogfight going on inside me, and the dog I feed is the dog that wins."

Think of it this way. Girls who are heavily into Madonna begin to dress and wear their hair like Madonna. If I listen to Pee Wee Herman or Eddie Murphy long enough I begin to talk like they talk. We all do it.

We are drawn toward the strong influences around us— and that isn't always good. But Paul tells us there is a way to get free. That's where Romans comes in. This book contains God's purpose for our lives: to conform us to the image of Christ (Romans 8:29). Romans tells us that:

1) the world is a mess because of sin (1:18–32);

2) so am I (chapter 2);

3) by faith in Christ the mess (my sin) is cleaned up, made right, and atoned for (3:21–28);

4) we need to understand our new spiritual condition (chapters 5 through 7);

5) and we have to realize that God really is in control and uses all things for good to draw us into his plan to conform us to his image (chapter 8).

Artist Billy Sprague is as he is because he's trying to be as God wants him.

How to make the right decision

■ *Tom Beard*

Have you ever faced a major decision that seemed so massive that you were afraid to decide one way or another? Maybe a dilemma that would result in changing the pattern or direction of your life?

I've had a few tough decisions like that in my life, too. I haven't always made the right choice, but I'm learning. What I've learned is some steps that help me make right decisions. Here they are:

Step One. *Don't worry or become anxious about your decision (Philippians 4:6–7).* God's concerned about what concerns you, so talk to him. He promises that if you do, his peace will guard your heart and mind in Christ.

He's going to stand guard, not letting anything in that doesn't have proper clearance (1 Peter 4:7)!

Step Two. *Look to God's Word for an example (Matthew 6:33–34).* There are thousands of scriptural examples dealing with godly people and what they did in their tough situations.

Granted, their decisions probably didn't involve cars, stereos, or new clothes. But most of life's toughies have already been covered. What did they do? How did it turn out? Was God honored by their decisions?

Almost any type of dilemma has already been dealt with, either successfully or disastrously. But, when possible, it's always better to learn from others' mistakes than to make your own (Hebrews 4:11).

Step Three. *Pray about*

■ ■ ■

it. I know, you already did this in step one, but do it again and this time concentrate on asking God to give you the strength to do what's right and godly.

Sometimes we're bothered by decisions because we just don't *want* to deny ourselves and choose what God wants. It's going to take a lot of determination and a desire to please God, but he rewards whoever looks for him (Hebrews 11:6 and Romans 12:2).

Step Four. *Make your decision, knowing that as you obey God and his Word, you're in his will.*

Sometimes this means deciding for God even if you don't have a clue how its going to turn out (Hebrews 11:8–10). But you don't *have* to know how everything is going to turn out. Your job is to honor God and admit he's in control, and

you'll be directed by his Spirit (Proverbs 3:6). And, as an added bonus, you'll live forever (1 John 2:17)!

So that's it—Tom's patented four-step process for making the right decision every time.

It's not easy, and it might be uncomfortable at times. But if you follow these steps, like I've been trying to do in my own life, you'll make better decisions and God will be glorified. And that, for Christians, should be a strong motivation.

■ *Tom Beard, formerly a keyboard player, vocalist, and songwriter for the band Glad, is now pursuing a solo career.*

DAY 32

■ ■ ■ The Unlovely

■ *Scott Wesley Brown*

The first time I went to Africa was during the height of the drought and famine.

We walked into the first village and saw the starving children. They were just as hungry for love as they were for food.

As I walked down the streets, kids began following me. Soon they were pressing in on all sides, reaching and grabbing me, trying to hold my hand and climb up on me.

I went through a terrible moment of fear. They were *too close*—I thought I might catch one of their many diseases. They had big open wounds. The flies that were swarming around their faces were beginning to land on me.

The smell was overpowering. I wanted to push them all away from me. But I seemed to hear Jesus say, "Scott, you're afraid to let them touch you.

But don't you realize that, despite your sin, sickness, and the wounds in your life, I touched you? I allowed you to get close to me."

As Christians, we need to be willing to lay down our lives, open up our hearts, to embrace humanity—even those we think are undesirables, the nerds, the down-and-outters.

God wants us to be like Jesus, who with open arms embraced all of humanity. With open arms, we need to do the same.

■ *Scott Wesley Brown is a Christian artist and founder of I Care, an international ministry of love and compassion.*

I'm In God's Hands

Renee Garcia

A few years ago I experienced a very down time. I felt I didn't count for anything and that I was just wandering aimlessly. I wondered if there was a plan for my life, but I didn't trust God.

Everybody else seemed to have more talents than I did. That made me wonder about myself and it made me wonder about God, who made me.

I had a romantic view of other Christians. I thought they never had any problems and I was amazed at how easy life seemed for them. I admired them, but they discouraged me because I couldn't be like they were.

Then a friend read this passage to me: "For I know the plans I have for you, plans to prosper you and not harm you, plans to give you hope and a future. Then you will call upon me and pray to me, and I will listen to you. You will seek me and find me when you seek me with all your heart" (Jeremiah 29:11–13).

I still have to ignore my feelings and doubts and remember to seek God. I still need to abandon my fears to him daily. I still need to trust him when I'm not sure where he's taking me.

But this passage, which is a promise from God, did give me the key I needed to unlock my heart, step outside my own feelings and insecurities, and begin to trust him with my life.

■ *Renee Garcia is a Christian singer who makes her home in Nashville.*

The biggest stumbling block

■ *Dana Key*

What's the biggest stumbling block in the world? What one thing causes more people to fall away from God than anything else?

It's not big-league sins like drugs, sex, lust, greed, envy, jealousy, or all the rest. Our biggest stumbling block is *guilt.* More than anything else, guilt keeps us from growing closer to the Lord day by day.

I've got news for you: everyone sins. That includes evil people who don't know God, and it includes Christians like you, me, Billy Graham, and everybody else—except Jesus.

But when Christians sin, Christ forgives us and helps us get back up again. It's like two wrestlers fighting it out. Sin may knock us down and trap us, but Christ helps us get up off the mat.

That's where the problem of guilt comes in. Guilt makes it hard to get up after we fall. Guilt makes us stay on the floor, feeling beat up and helpless.

I've been a Christian for over ten years, but there's still something in me that makes me want to run from God when I sin. It tells me, "Dana, you can't face God now, can you?"

The same thing happened to Adam and Eve in the third chapter of Genesis. Because they felt guilty, they hid from God after eating the fruit he had told them to stay away from. People have been hiding from God ever since.

Where does all this guilt come from? If TV's Church Lady were here, she'd probably say, "Oh, I don't know. Maybe ... S - A - T - A - N ?"

■ ■ ■

The Bible tells us that one of the names of Satan is the slanderer. People in America can be sued for slandering another person, but Satan gets by with it all the time.

Satan slanders God by whispering things in our ear like "God doesn't really love you," or "God can't really forgive you for *this!*" Satan also slanders us by saying "You can't be a Christian if you sin like this," or "Come on. You've committed this sin so many times you're hopeless. Give up."

I believe these lies sometimes myself—but I try to fight it. Here's how:

First, I confess my sins to God every day. God promises that, if we do that, he'll forgive us (1 John 1:9). I make confession a regular part of my prayer and Bible reading time. That way I am cleansed from guilt every day and I don't have to carry all that garbage around with me all the time.

Second, I confess my sins to other people. This can be rough, I know. But sometimes God seems to be urging me to confess my sin to a person I may have hurt by my sin. I confess it to the person I have offended, and then go back to God and pray.

It's hard to admit it when we're wrong. When you're lying on the floor, it's hard to cry out to God and ask him to help you get back up. But that's the only way we can fight the stumbling block of guilt.

■ *Dana Key believes you can confess sin to God anywhere. He first did it in a janitor's closet at his high school in Memphis!*

Wrestling with God

■ *John Elliott*

Some people take their relationship with God pretty casually. Sometimes I do it myself. But a look at Jacob's life can remind us that our relationship with God can be very real if we take it seriously.

Jacob's relationship with God was so real that God visited him. In fact, God (or one of his angels) once had a wrestling match with Jacob (Genesis 32:22–32). That's pretty real.

Think about prayer for a minute. There are times when it becomes intense—like when we want something badly (such as a change in our life or freedom from temptation) or when we realize something bad about ourselves that we want to change.

Jacob wasn't just wrestling with God that night—he was also wrestling with himself. He knew that he was a selfish, de-ceptive person. In fact, his name meant deceiver. But Jacob wanted God's blessing so badly that he wrestled all night, refusing to let go until God blessed him.

Compared to Jacob, we let go too easily in prayer. We don't persevere. Jacob really hung on, and God honored that.

Sometimes we think prayer is for old people who don't have anything better to do, but history shows that some of the great prayer movements and re-vivals in the church have been started by young people; later, the adults caught on.

Recently I was at Purdue University, where 500 students got together on a Fri-day night—and about 600 on Saturday—just to pray. They were from many different de-nominations, and all the different

campus organizations. But they were unified; they knew what they were coming for.

Saturday night we prayed for over two hours—without any top-name Christian bands or anything!

In Nashville, some of us have been meeting and praying together for about a year. Last Thursday morning, 40 people came out at 5:30 a.m. to pray. That's exciting! And I believe this is all a prelude to a nation-wide revival.

Why is this happening? Because God is calling his people to wrestle with him. It's not some great idea we've come up with—but we're still clinging to him, saying "We won't let you go until you send a revival."

It's tough to pray sometimes. Our culture is so busy and so noisy that it's hard for us to quiet ourselves before God. But if we wrestle with God in prayer, he will bless us. That's his promise.

■ *John Elliott is a pianist, songwriter, and record producer who lives in Nashville.*

Solo Christians

■ *James Ward*

Our society is very individualistic. People believe they have to do things on their own, whether it's our Michael Jackson singing "I'm Bad" or our parents' Frank Sinatra singing "I Did It My Way."

It's been this way for a long time. Think of the image of the western cowboy, at home— but all alone—on the range.

Today, our individualism is leading some people to get wrapped up in developing and perfecting their own bodies. They exercise and work out, trying to push their body farther and farther—while they fall deeper and deeper into solitude and self-centeredness.

Unfortunately, this individualism may be leading us to ignore an important part of being a Christian: our gathering together.

God tells us, "Let us consider how we may spur one another on toward love and good deeds. Let us not give up meeting together, as some are in the habit of doing, but let us encourage one another—and all the more as you see the Day approaching" (Hebrews 10:24–25).

Jesus showed us the way. Many people think of Jesus as a solitary, lonely man. But most of his ministry was public—leading his disciples, teaching the multitudes, and reaching out to the needy.

Likewise, the early church was known for its commitment to "the apostles' teaching and to the fellowship, to the breaking of bread and to prayer" (Acts 2:42). They met together, and they reached out to others.

Don't get me wrong—I

■ ■ ■

know how school activities can make it hard to get involved in church. Kids are active in organizations, sports activities, drama, music, and other things—and many of them feel driven to be the best in these areas.

In high school, I couldn't be in band because rehearsal was on a night I was involved at church. Some of the kids in my church group hardly ever showed up—they were too busy developing their skills as musicians or athletes. Unfortunately, many of them became lukewarm in their faith. Their skills and their personal disciplines replaced the priorities of fellowship and meeting with other believers.

And there are other reasons people don't fellowship together. One couple at my church got so involved romantically they no longer "had time" for church. And some just aren't *aware* that God wants us

to fellowship. Others simply don't want to. Some kids may be incompatible with other people at church. Or some secret sin may drive a wedge between one believer and other believers.

But problems and challenges like these should really cause us to pull together rather than pull apart.

Sometimes Christians remind me of the song, "Me and Jesus, we got a good thing goin'." There's nothing wrong with having a good thing going with Jesus, but God wants us to get other people involved in our Christian life, too.

■ *James Ward travels constantly, but he is actively involved in New City Fellowship in Chattanooga, Tennessee.*

A hymn to Christ

■ *Michael Card*

"Who being in very nature God did not consider equality with God something to be grasped, but made himself nothing, taking the very nature of a servant, being made in human likeness. And being found in appearance as a man, he humbled himself and became obedient to death—even death on a cross! Therefore God exalted him to the highest place and gave him the name that is above every name, that at the name of Jesus every knee should bow, in heaven and on earth and under the earth, and every tongue confess that Jesus Christ is Lord, to the glory of God the Father" (Philippians 2:6–11).

The Bible is full of poems and songs. When Adam first saw Eve, he responded with a poem. When Simeon finally held the promised Messiah in his arms, his prophetic words came out in song. Here in Philippians Paul celebrates who Jesus is in a hymn—a hymn that seems to have one verse and a chorus.

The verse describes what God was truly like when he came into the world through Christ. The chorus celebrates the result of his coming.

The verse focuses on two attributes: humility and servanthood. Christ might have claimed equality with God—but instead, as we read in verse 7, he made himself nothing. If we are to portray the image of God in our lives, then we too must, as Paul tells us in Ephesians 4:2, "Be completely humble and gentle."

The second trait is servanthood—"taking the very nature

of a servant," Paul says of Christ in verse 7.

Jesus tells us that he did not come to be served, but to serve (Matthew 20:28). He was a true servant, washing feet and fixing meals. Even after his resurrection he prepared breakfast for his followers who had been up all night (John 21). He instucts us to become servants as well (Matthew 20:26).

But this hymn is not about humility or servanthood. They are only expressions of the real subject of this passage: the *obedience* of Christ, who "became obedient to death, even death on a cross!"

This is radical obedience, and it is the kind that he desires from us. Hebrews speaks of his obedience with the fantastic phrase, "he learned obedience through what he suffered" (5:8). Elsewhere in Hebrews, Christ's attitude is described: "I have come to do your will, O God" (10:7). If Jesus' life was about anything, it was about obedience.

And because of Christ's humility and obedience, God exalted him (v. 9). In the radical reversal of the Kingdom of God, the suffering servant turns out to be the Lord of Glory, and the most humble one turns out to be the exalted one—all because of his obedience.

This same radical reversal can take place in our own lives. We are told that whoever humbles himself will be exalted (Luke 14:11, James 4:10), and that he who would be first must be the servant of all.

Let servanthood and humility abound in your life as the expression of your obedience to Christ who lives through you.

Michael Card is a Christian singer, songwriter, and musician whose songs carry meaty messages.

DAY 38

■ ■ ■ Four Steps to Jesus

■ *Mike Warnke*

Being a Christian isn't complicated, even though we try to make it that way sometimes.

I've found a simple, four-step formula that will help you live a successful Christian life.

1. *Be available.* God can't use you if you're too busy to hear his call or to do what he wants. Make yourself available to God, even if that means setting aside time every day to more closely follow him.

2. *Be in love with Jesus.* Learn to spend time with Jesus daily in prayer, meditation, and study of the Word. Your love and devotion to Christ will spill out into your life.

3. *Be in love with the people around you.* If you really love Jesus, you'll feel the hurt he feels when people are suffering.

4. *Be confident in the talents God has given you.* Don't be afraid to be yourself, and be willing to give the talents that you have back to God.

Follow these four steps— and then get ready for anything, because God can use you!

■ *Christian comic Mike Warnke has been making himself available to speak and teach for over seventeen years now.*

Play to Win

Ken Davis

Imagine a football coach giving his team this pep talk:

"Okay, boys—we haven't got a chance today. The other team is against us, and the officials favor them. So just try to keep the other team from scoring. If you feel any pain, just quit."

That team would never win a game. To win, you have to have a positive attitude; you have to want to move the ball forward.

Can that positive attitude help you with the challenges you face at home, getting along with your parents, brothers, and sisters? Yes, it can—if you learn to apply it to three areas of your life.

First, *have a positive concept of yourself.* See yourself as a giantkiller. You're not a helpless child—you're the child of a king. Because of him, you can accomplish the impossible.

Second, *develop a positive attitude toward your family.* Look for the good in your family, and you'll find things you never knew existed (see Philippians 4:4–8).

Third, *think positively about the future.* Decide to show your family the love of Christ in every way you can. Be aggressive!

No matter how difficult things are at home, look at that challenge the way David looked at Goliath: as an opportunity— for slingshot practice.

 *This discussion was adapted from Ken Davis's newest book:* How to Live with Your Parents Without Losing Your Mind *(Zondervan, 1988).*

Lifestyles of the rich and nameless

■ *Dan Ruple*

It's fun to watch the TV shows about the rich people and all their cars, houses, pools, and hot tubs. But in Luke 18:18–27, there's a story about a rich man who met Jesus, and Jesus was not impressed.

The guy came walking up to Jesus and asked, "How can I inherit eternal life?" He already had everything else, so he probably wanted a gold-plated key to heaven, too.

Jesus took a minute to check the guy out. "What about the Ten Commandments?" asked Jesus. The guy shot right back: "I've kept them since my youth."

Nowadays, if we met a guy like that we'd think he was pretty amazing. And sometimes we do run into non-Christians who seem to be naturally more honest and good than some of us Christians who pray about it and work on it all the time. But with Jesus, having it all together still doesn't count for righteousness.

Next Jesus tested the top priorities in the rich man's life. He could see that this guy's heart was totally wrapped up in his possessions, so Jesus threw him a curve ball: "Go and sell all you have and give it to the poor and follow me."

It's not sinful to be wealthy. The problem was that this guy had let money and possessions become the most important things in his life. He had no identity outside of his riches; in fact, today we know him only as "the rich young ruler." He doesn't have a name like Dan or Bob. That's why I call this devotional "Lifestyles of the Rich and Nameless.'' He had lost his personal unique identity.

We're quick to look at the outside. If someone is rich, youthful, or energetic, we admire that. But Jesus is saying that the outside doesn't matter—it's the inside that counts.

When I first got saved I was a big movie and music buff. I'd go to three movies a week, and I had a huge record collection. But I felt God urging me to put these things away for a while—not because they are evil, but because they were too important in my life. Later on, when I had a better handle on these things, I began going to movies and buying records again.

Before I became a Christian, I was known as the class clown. It was easy to hide behind my funny facade and not show myself. But when the Lord came into my life, it was as if he said, ''I want to make you a well-rounded person—not just a phony facade.''

Let's avoid trying to be famous and ending up nameless. Let's allow the Lord to develop our inward qualities and not be obsessed with outer things like hair, clothes, money, cars, and our bodies.

Let's get rid of our facades. Let's turn over to the Lord the things that are too important to us. Then, we can be what God really created us to be.

Dan Ruple is a radio deejay on station KBRT in Costa Mesa, California.

Fearing God

■ *Al Menconi*

People don't like to feel fear. It's no fun thinking that somebody may sneak up on you and hit you or rob you.

But that's not what we mean when we talk about fearing God. Proverbs 1:7 says, "The fear of the Lord is the beginning of knowledge." Does God want us to be afraid of him? I don't think so.

A better word to explain what God means by fearing him is "reverence."

I learned what reverence meant in college. After classes, we used to surf at a spot between Huntington Beach and Newport Beach. We called it "the wedge" because waves from two different directions would come together, forming a mountain-sized wave that would slam the surfers onto the beach. Only the really crazy surfers would go out there and try the wedge.

I wasn't that crazy—I used to go there just to watch the crazy guys surf. But one day, some girls near me were watching their boyfriends surf, saying, "Oh, look at Pete surf!" "Look at that wild man Bill!" "Look at Frank take that wave!"

I can surf as good as those guys, I thought. I had been surfing on three-, four-, and five-foot waves; these waves looked about that size. *I can handle them.*

I meandered into the water, making sure the girls noticed me.

When you surf, there's something called the *surf line,* the perfect place to sit on your board waiting to catch the wave. As I sat, my legs dangling in the water, a set

■ ■ ■

of waves began to come in. The closer they got, the more they swelled; they got bigger and bigger. When they were twenty feet away, I panicked.

I dove as deep as I could go and let the first wave break over me. After the second wave, I turned my board around and started paddling back toward the beach on the white water. It took me 45 minutes to paddle in 50 yards.

When I finally got back to the beach I fell down, exhausted. (Luckily I was far enough down the beach that the girls didn't see me struggling in.) I dried off and lay on the sand, watching my friends ride the waves I couldn't ride.

T hose waves hadn't looked so big—or scary—from the sand. But when I got out close to them, I understood their majesty. Their

power. Their force. I learned to respect—or *reverence*—those waves because of their power.

The Bible talks about reverence in the same way. Sitting on the beach of life, we look at God as the big policeman or babysitter in the sky. We think, *Hey—I can handle God.* But when we draw closer to him, we see his power and majesty. Then we understand what it means to reverence God. That kind of reverence for God is the first step to wisdom.

■ *Between surfing and other experiences on the beach, Al Menconi did actually attend classes at Pasadena City College.*

Serving God in the midst of our lives

■ *Margaret Becker*

God calls us to serve him—but our lives are full of things like studying, going to work, washing clothes, and fixing meals. How do we fit it all in?

Like this: We should serve God, honor God, and get our inspiration and strength from God first. What time remains we'll need for the details of life.

A pastor in New York said we ought to tithe our time like we tithe our money. That would give God something like 17 prayer and fellowship hours every week! Think about that for a minute. If we were to spend even a substantial portion of that time before God, waiting, persisting in prayer until we know that he has spoken to us, we'd have a focus for the rest of our life.

I tested this approach when I was in college. I was absolutely terrible in chemistry, so I hired a tutor and spent hours and hours studying, but I still couldn't grasp it.

The night before the final exam, a friend called me. He was going through a very difficult time; he was very upset and asked me to come over to talk and pray with him. "Sorry—no way," I said. I couldn't flunk this exam.

As soon as I hung up I was convicted. This man was talking about his life. I was talking about an exam. I prayed, "I know that life is more important than an exam. I have prepared all I can for this test. Now, in obedience to you, I'll go talk to my friend."

Late that night I came home, did a little more studying, and went to bed.

I showed up in the morning for my exam and realized that I'd forgotten one thing—my calculator. I couldn't buy one or borrow one, so on top of everything else I had to do the whole chemistry exam longhand.

I got an A+ on the exam and an A for the course.

I'm not saying you can just blow off schoolwork. Just the opposite—I had really put 100% into it up to that point. But the Lord showed me two things: First, that laying down your life for a friend is more important than an exam. And second, when he directs you, you must be obedient to him. He will make up the difference in the details.

I'm still wrestling with this issue. My life is full of details every day, and when I kneel down to pray, those details come racing into my head. I have a notepad there to write them down so that I don't let them distract me, and then I go on praying.

When I finish praying, I don't always have time for all those details—but none of those I've missed so that I could spend time with the Lord has ever come to a disastrous ending. God is gracious, and he will make up for lost details.

Christian artist Margaret Becker is tending to the details of a growing recording and concert ministry.

DAY 43

■ ■ ■ God's Plan

■ *Phil Madeira*

Life is full of surprises. It's impossible to predict what's coming at you from around the corner.

We should all have plans, but we have to be ready when things don't go as planned. It's a good idea to start the day knowing that someone might misjudge you or mistreat you—maybe mistakenly, maybe even on purpose.

We can't control those situations, but we *can* control how we're going to respond. God says, ''What does the Lord require of you but to do justice, to love kindness, and to walk humbly with your God'' (Micah 6:8).

When something wrong comes our way, we are to be people of justice, not harsh judges. We're to be merciful to the guy who doesn't treat us as we expect him to.

We are told to walk humbly before God—not to walk around with our face toward the ground thinking we're nothing, but to know that we are imperfect people that God dearly loves.

You'll make some mistakes today. When you do, make that verse your prayer, as I have done. It will help you remember that God loves you, that he forgives you for your mistakes, and that he'll help you act justly and mercifully to everyone around you.

■ *Phil Madeira is singer, songwriter, keyboard whiz, and pretty nice guy.*

Faking It

Duffy Robbins

I read a story in the paper the other day about a 28-year old guy named Mark Carver who worked as a doctor and as an assistant medical director.

The problem was that Mark had never gone to college or medical school. He allegedly forged documents to get the job as a doctor. If convicted, he'll spend seven years in jail.

Mark reminds me of a lot of people I know who call themselves Christians. They look like Christians. They go to church. They don't swear or drink a lot. They pray once in a while. But they're just going through the motions—they've never made a personal commitment to Christ.

Paul says that, in the last days, "people will be lovers of themselves, lovers of money, boastful, proud, abusive, disobedient to their parents, ungrateful, unholy, without love, unforgiving, slanderous, without self-control, brutal, not lovers of the good, treacherous, rash, conceited, lovers of pleasure rather than lovers of God" (2 Timothy 3:1–5). Phew! What a list! He also says that many people will have a form of religion while denying God's power. In other words, they look like Christians but they ain't.

I wouldn't want a phony doctor operating on me. And God doesn't need any phony Christians. If you've been going through the motions and acting like you're a Christian, why not accept Christ and make it real?

Duffy Robbins, who is a professor at Eastern College and writes tons of books, did actually go to college and get a degree!

God says: "Cool out!"

■ *Randy Stonehill*

We all have stress and anxiety in our lives. It's part of modern life, right?

There are a couple of things that make my life especially stressful. First, I live in Los Angeles, which is one of the busiest, most heavily populated cities on earth. Second is my vocation as a musical communicator.

If what I do on stage is going to have the ring of truth, I must be vulnerable to God and vulnerable to the audience. If I want him to lead me, I have to be willing to let him come close to me. If I want to be the best servant I can be during a concert, I have to relinquish control to him—and be willing to go where he takes me.

For me, this is an emotionally intense tightrope between "being professional" and walking

in faith. My pride and my livelihood are at stake—which definitely opens me up to fear and anxiety.

About ten years ago, I was really feeling the tension. I was starting to dread my work. The more successful I became, the more tense and frightened of failure I became.

One particular portion of Scripture became really central to my life at that time, and has been ever since: "Do not be anxious about anything, but in everything, by prayer and petition, present your requests to God. And the peace of God, which transcends all understanding, will guard your hearts and your minds in Christ Jesus" (Philippians 4:6–7).

How outrageous! I thought at first. *How can anyone say that? This person obviously*

doesn't understand life in modern America!

Then I remembered: *Hey—this is God talking. He understands exactly what is going on, and if he says have no anxiety, he means it. He's the only one with the right to say things like that.*

God is the only one who's really in control, and he'll be there to give me the strength and peace that passes all understanding—if I choose to obey and trust him.

Now, when I truly release a concert to him before I walk on stage I experience a full-throttled freedom and joy. I'm freed by realizing that I don't have to live up to anything, not even being "one of the pioneers of contemporary Christian music." My ultimate responsibility to God, the audience, and myself is to try my very best to be all God has made me to be,

one day at a time, and to walk in faith.

I still struggle with anxiety, but these days I'm winning far more than I'm losing.

Those verses in Philippians are God's promise for all of us. God has control of your life, the struggles you're having with parents and friends, the trials you're facing at school, and all your fears and doubts and insecurities.

Philippians 4, verses 6 and 7, is God's way of saying: "Excuse me, but I'm in control here. So please trust me and cool out!"

Whether he can handle the pressure or not, Randy Stonehill is one of the pioneers of contemporary Christian music.

DAY 46

■ ■ ■ God's Hot-shots

■ *Ed DeGarmo*

Want to know what drives me nuts? It's when people come up to me and Dana after a concert and say, "Boy, if the Lord would give me a platform like you guys, I could really serve the Lord!"

People don't need to be popular musicians, big-time preachers, rich business people, famous actors, top-name authors, or hot-shot TV stars so they can use their fame and status to serve God.

God's definition of success is different from ours. We think of money and fame; God's definition of success is found in the fruit of the Spirit (Galatians 5:22–23).

God wants us to serve him where we are. As Paul told Timothy: "Do not neglect your gift" (1 Timothy 4:14). Your gift may be in accounting, or in laying bricks or in praying for leaders and missionaries around the world. Those things won't make you famous, but God's work depends on those skills. If we are faithful in these things, God will take care of the rest.

When you see a concert, hear a record, or listen to a sermon by a "famous" preacher, don't think, *If only I could be that person.* Ask God to reveal your gifts and abilities to you; then use them to serve God with all your strength.

■ *Early in his career, Ed DeGarmo, a founder of the band DeGarmo & Key, quit playing music for a few years to serve God in other ways.*

Pray for the Punks

Bill Walden

One night as our band was packing up after a concert, four kids in black, with punk haircuts and lots of studs and dark makeup, began harassing us. When they learned we were a Christian band, they really gave us a hard time.

We weren't getting anywhere talking to them in the parking lot; besides, we were hungry. We offered to buy them a hamburger.

At MacDonald's, their attitude began to soften. Soon, we realized that their hardness was just a shell to protect them; inside, they were hurting.

One girl's father had beaten her since she was small. One of the guys said his parents didn't care what he did as long as he didn't make too much noise or go to jail. They were only in their teens, but already they had experienced enough sadness and sorrow for someone five times their age.

We told them about ourselves; we told them what God meant to us. As we left MacDonald's, they said, "Hey, you guys are OK." There was no dramatic salvation scene. They didn't give their lives to Christ. But we thanked God for letting us talk to them that night.

There may be kids in your school who are different from you, who are trying to be hard. Take a chance—show them a little love. It may be the only love they've seen that day—or that year.

■ *Before joining Mirrors, Bill Walden sang for Undercover.*

You're worth a lot

■ *Fred J. Heumann*

Who is worth more, you or the pastor of your church? Here's a fun one to ask Americans: Who's worth more, the President of the United States or the Ayatollah of Iran? Or what about former President John Kennedy or Lee Harvey Oswald, the man who assassinated him?

The answer: All of these people are equally valuable in God's sight. That's hard for us to imagine because our values have been shaped by society's value system, rather than God's.

Like society around us, many Christians fall into the trap of evaluating people according to the *4 P's:* personal appearance, performance, position, and possessions.

These things are important to a degree, but they don't determine our values. I call them

false boxtops. It's like someone giving you a jigsaw puzzle, only they've swapped the lids on the puzzle boxes. So you try to put the pieces together, only they don't match the picture that's on the box.

To avoid that, we need a Biblical world view. A good place to start is Genesis 1:26–27, which tells us that we have been created in the image of God. We don't physically look like God, but the part of us that liasts is.

Later in that chapter, it tells us that God looked at all he had made and said it was very good. That includes you and me. That doesn't mean we're perfect. Some time later, Adam and Eve sinned, and we've been sinning ever since. Some people conclude that, because of sin, we're totally

■ ■ ■

worthless. That's what I call "worm theology," the belief that we're just poor worms, not worth anything. We are *unworthy*—but we're not worthless.

Don't fall into the trap of looking at people who are unbelievers as heathen scum. God sees them as valuable. And we should, too. That really is our motivation for evangelism: the value that God has placed on these people.

If you had a price tag, it wouldn't say five dollars or even a million dollars. It would say, "Jesus." Jesus was the price that God paid—not just for me but the guy next door, the dope addict in the inner city, the gang leader, or the "nice" businessman who takes bribes on the side.

Let's not value ourselves by the 4 P's. Our value comes from God. We're not totally good or totally bad. We're both wonderful *and* wicked. Let's learn to value ourselves and everyone we come in contact with just as much as God does, and tell them how priceless they are to him.

■ *Fred Heumann loves people, and not just because his name is pronounced "human."*

89

What God wants

■ *Ken Davis*

Asking what God wants is really a simple way of asking, "What is God's will for my life?" Young people struggle with hundreds of questions: Should I go to this school or that school? Should I date this guy or that girl? But those things will fall into place if we understand what God really wants. And what God really wants is explained in Romans 12:1–2.

The first thing God wants is your body. When I was a child I sang the song, "Oh, be careful little hands what you do." At fourteen, it's uncool to sing those songs—they're too childish. But that song pinpoints how we can know God's will better than anything else. In fact, earlier in Romans we are told to dedicate our hands and our lips as instruments to be used by God.

God wants your body. It's easy to say, *I give God my life*—that's nice and vague. It's much harder to give him your body, because you care very much about your body. You spend a lot of time in front of the mirror making sure it looks right, you feed it when it's hungry, and you pamper it when it hurts. And God wants it.

Paul put it another way when he told us to "give our bodies as a living sacrifice." That made me chuckle the first time I read it, because when the Israelites sacrificed animals, there weren't a lot of sheep that came back from the sacrifices. The sheep were totally consumed. But God doesn't want just a dead sacrifice, he wants a living sacrifice.

■ ■ ■

It's easy to keep a dead sheep on the sacrifice fire, but a living sacrifice has the option of crawling off the altar at any time. We have that choice every day, and every minute. But if we really want to do what God wants we will choose each day to stay there and allow our body to be used for his purposes.

Christianity is not just a list of rules or dos and don'ts. It's having a relationship with the living God. And our behavior at work, school, on a date, or in the locker room would be significantly different if he were our partner and companion in each of those situations. The interesting thing is that he *is* our partner there with us, and we need to be aware of that—always.

After God has our body—our hands, feet, sexuality and everything—there's one other thing he wants: our will.

Romans tells us, "Be not conformed to this world." That means our lives are not directed by the people around us (neither our church friends nor our school friends) or by circumstances. Rather, our lives are directed by God.

He wants us to say to him, "Lord, the purpose of my life is to live for you." That's hard, because we're committing ourselves to something that we don't totally understand, and that takes trust. But God is worth our trust, our lives, our bodies, and our wills.

When we do these things, it will be easier for us to decide who to date, what to do, and how to act, because he will be acting through us.

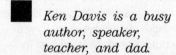 *Ken Davis is a busy author, speaker, teacher, and dad.*

God can do it, if you let him

■ *Robin Crow*

I was on tour in Montana when God revealed himself to me in a humbling, miraculous way.

A week before the tour, I had taken a fall while jumping on a trampoline, throwing out my back. Even so, I couldn't resist indulging in my passion for riding horses when I got to Montana. After all, Montana is horse heaven. They're everywhere!

Between concerts, the pastor of a small Spanish-speaking church heard I was in the area and tracked me down at my hotel. His opening words were, "We don't have any money, and most of the congregation doesn't speak English. But we would be so blessed if you would come play for us."

How could I say no to that?

I arrived in Billings, Montana, on the day I was to play at the Spanish church. It was a beautiful Sunday, so naturally I spent the afternoon racing across the countryside on horseback with some folks who raised Arabian pedigrees.

That was the straw that broke the camel's back, so to speak. By the time I arrived at the church, I was in such pain that I had to be helped out of the car.

I couldn't walk. I couldn't even stand up, and that's no exaggeration. All I could think of was how good it would feel to be back at the hotel soaking in a steaming hot tub.

But the congregation had different ideas—they decided that God was going to heal me right on the spot.

As they brought me up

■ ■ ■

front and started praying over me in Spanish, I was wishing I could be anywhere else. But then the pastor laid his hand on me—and a light, burning sensation shot down my spine. I stood straight up.

And that was all there was to it. I had been healed. I had been physically touched by God—no if's, and's, or but's. I've always been a doubting Thomas when it comes to dramatic spiritual miracles, even though for years I've hungered and prayed and waited for a touch from God. In the end, it happened in his timing and in a most unexpected setting.

So be encouraged. God is alive and well. He speaks Spanish and has been hanging out in Montana.

P.S.: Take heart. If you've ever experienced doubt in your walk with the Lord, remember that his light will brighten your way when you least expect it— and when you need it most.

■ *Guitarist Robin Crow has a large repertoire of instrumental music that can be understood in any language.*

DAY 51

■ ■ ■ Our "Supplier"

■ *Ian Tanner*

When we pray, we need to show God that we mean business.

We don't take prayer seriously. We take it easy; we say, "Lord, I need this. Thanks. See you later."

I don't think God wants us to pretend to be super-spiritual. He loves us as we are. But when we ask for something, I think we should ask with all our hearts.

Jesus said, "Ask and it will be given to you; seek and you will find; knock and the door will be opened to you. For everyone who asks receives; he who seeks finds; and to him who knocks, the door will be opened" (Luke 11:9–10).

God *wants* to give us things. He is our friend, our heavenly Father, and our "supplier." He has promised to give us the things that we need—

but we need to have the right attitude first. Sometimes we don't receive because we don't care enough about what we're seeking.

For example: I have to pray about spiritual growth a lot. I don't want to become stagnant—but I start to get stagnant if I don't pray hard and often about growing spiritually. It's the same with other things, too. We need to ask, seek, knock, and knock some more.

■ *Ian Tanner is a member of the Canadian band* The Awakening.

What's the Big Idea?

Billy Sprague

Jesus is God. That is the most radical, most powerful idea in the history of mankind.

There have been other important ideas, of course, some of them good and some of them evil. Some of them have changed people's behavior. Because of the ideas of modern physicians, sick people now take pills and shots instead of incantations and home remedies. When Hitler distorted Neitzsche's philosophy into an idea about a perfect race, he killed millions of people trying to fulfill that idea.

But as I try to figure out life, the single idea that makes the most sense and the most impact is the idea that Jesus is God.

I had a chance to check out this idea back in 1971 when some surgery put me on my back for nine months. I had heard about Jesus, but I had never checked it out for myself. So I read about him in the Bible—and I found truth that changed me forever.

The fact that Jesus is God answers all our big questions. We can know who we are, where we came from, and where we fit into the cosmic scheme of things. We can find love and purpose in a world of big, weird, and often bogus ideas.

So what's the big idea? Jesus is God. It doesn't get any bigger than that.

■ *Billy Sprague is a former youth worker who got the big idea to become a musical artist.*

Peer pressure
■ *Michael Peace*

All this talk about peer pressure is missing the point. The worst pressure on teenagers doesn't come from other teenagers—it comes from adults.

Take alcohol. If a 15-year-old kid goes into a bar and gets drunk, he has definitely done something he shouldn't. And so have the adults who let him come into the bar in the first place, and who sold him the stuff.

Look at the wine coolers that kids are drinking. Those aren't being made and marketed by kids. They're from adults who deliberately advertise the stuff to kids.

What about the pressure to look and dress sexy? Kids aren't designing and marketing those clothes.

The same goes for ob-scene records and movies. The record and movie companies aren't run by children—they're run by adults to make money. Right now those companies are making a lot of money from kids. But the sad thing is that they're also affecting kids' behavior—in a very negative way.

Things have gotten so bad that I've gone on something I call a crusade of rebellion. I'm teaching kids to rebel against the whole system of exploitation of children by greedy or evil people.

Don't get me wrong: This is not a full-fledged war against adults. After all, I'm an adult myself!

What I'm trying to do is help kids understand that some of the pressure on them goes against the will of God— whether it's pressures from

■ ■ ■

adults or pressures from kids their own age. I'm telling them to watch out for what they're opening themselves up to.

When a kid (or anyone else) sins, he is responsible for that sin. We're not just victims. If we believe we're just victims, that it's not really our fault, we think that gives us permission to continue doing what we're doing. That's not right.

So how can you join me in my crusade of rebellion?

First, look at the Bible. Compare what kids are doing now to what the Bible says, and you'll see that there are many things going on that are not pleasing to the Lord. If you want to please your Creator, you'll have to rebel against the wrong things that people are doing.

Then say yes to God. Say yes to his will. Say yes to his commands. If we say yes to God and say no to evil, we can avoid peer pressure of all kinds and do what God wants us to do.

■ *Michael Peace says "yes" and all sorts of things on his two Christian rap records.*

DAY 54

... I'm Falling

■ *Morgan Cryar*

When I was four or five years old, I went fishing with my dad. I wandered too far and fell into the water.

I was totally helpless—I don't remember even reaching out for help. But my dad dropped his pole, came running, and pulled me out of the water.

That was such a scary experience I'll never forget it. But since then I have thought about it in a new way, because God has saved me like that many times, by reaching down and picking me up when I was totally helpless.

He forgives me when I'm not worthy of that forgiveness. And he accepts me as I am, even when I fall again and again. He does more than forgive me: He shows he cares about me when I am totally helpless to earn his love.

Sometimes, when we feel helpless, we're more aware of the sensation of drowning than we are of God's reaching down to save us. But at times like that we need to remember that God is our Father, and that he knows what we're going through—and that he'll keep us from drowning.

■ *Christian artist Morgan Cryar is a father himself now.*

Slaves

Bryan Duncan

Jesus loves us and came to give us life more abundantly. Unfortunately, even after accepting Jesus, many of us remain slaves to our sins.

Let's face it. We sin every day. And when we sin, God's plan for our life is hindered. Through continuing in sin we miss God's highest plan for our lives. We're hurting ourselves.

There are cases of this in the Bible. Saul was a man God chose to be the first king over Israel. He was anointed by God, and he was young, strong, and outstanding. He was the best man in all Israel.

But after he had been king for a while, he became overconfident. He began exercising his power carelessly. Soon he was deliberately disobeying God; in fact, he became so disobedient God regretted ever choosing him.

Saul could have been an even greater king, but by continuing in sin he became a "Could-Have-Been." God chose another man to lead Israel. Saul's sin made him less than he could have been. He hurt himself.

Sure, God forgives us if we repent. But if we flee evil we will have the highest, most rewarding, most exciting life God has planned for us.

Remember: Our obedience is the controlling factor in God's plan for our lives.

■ *Bryan Duncan, cofounder of Sweet Comfort band, now sings records and sings solo.*

Flexing our spiritual muscles

■ *Rick Cua*

One thing that we as Christian believers need to do is flex the spiritual muscles the Lord has given us.

When we accepted Christ, Christ came to dwell within us. That means there's a lot of power available to us. But not many of us tap into that power—we either don't know it's there or we don't believe it.

Everyone is frightened by something. With some people it's moving, going to a new city and a new school—or maybe it's that first job interview.

For me, the scariest thing in school was to get up in front of the class and give a speech. To stand there for 15 or 20 minutes with 20 kids looking at me like I'm some kind of a dummy—I would be a real basket case, stuttering and stammering.

Since then I've learned about using the power God gives us. Now, when things frighten me, that's an opportunity to rely on God's power.

Now that you know you have this power, how are you going to use it?

There are only two ways to respond when we're confronted with something that's bigger than us. We can turn around and run away and not deal with the problem at all. We can go away and be "safe."

Or we can grab the bull by the horns—we can face the situation head on. We just might plow right through it. In other words, we need to flex the muscles that Jesus has given us.

Maybe, like me, you need to get up in front of people and tell them about the Lord. Maybe

■ ■ ■

the Lord's done something in your life—something spectacular like a miracle, or something more commonplace but still important—and you feel God saying "Hey, get up and give a testimonial to your youth group or church."

When those scary feelings come, when you feel afraid, jump to your feet! Grab the bull by the horns. Flex your muscles. The only way to overcome that fear is by facing it—with the power Christ has given you.

I'm getting to the point that, the more something scares me, the more I want to confront it. That's a big change for me—I used to want to run, and the more I ran, the easier it became to hide from my fears. But once I start tackling this stuff, I find myself saying, "Bring it on!

Come on—make my day!" It's not a matter of pride. It's just that I know that's what Christ wants. He doesn't want us to be fearful.

And Christ should get the glory for it, not us! But if we do it for him, we will be blessed. Absolutely! Too many of us are running from our fears, letting the devil control us through those fears. Let's flex our muscles—and fight back.

■ *Rick Cua has never done an exercise video with Jane Fonda, but his album "Wear Your Colors" does contain the song, "Flex."*

Wrestling with the enemy

■ John Elliott

In the Bible we're told that, "We wrestle not with flesh and blood, but against principalities and powers" (Ephesians 6:12). How does this wrestling with evil powers take place?

People have some funny ideas about Satan, our enemy. Some think he's the guy with the red suit and the pitchfork. Others ignore him altogether, which may be worse.

It's easy to get confused, because Satan works in an invisible realm. But just because it's invisible doesn't make it any less real. I believe that if we could see what was really taking place around us all the time in the angelic and demonic realm, we would be totally blown away.

We don't have to know everything about Satan, but we should know this: he is very subtle and he's constantly speaking to us.

One of Satan's main weapons is deception, and it works like this: a whole lake of pure water can be made deadly with just a pint of poison. Satan likes to work that way—he likes to feed us a lot of truth, a whole lake of truth and good things, with just a little poison mixed in.

He uses the good things in our lives as decoys. He wouldn't feed us a whole lake of poison because we would see what he was up to, but a small dose—nicely concealed in pure water—might fool us.

Satan also uses voices. We hear many voices in life—voices from our friends, relatives, and people at school. But the voices we hear are not necessarily the voice of God.

■ ■ ■

Satan often tries to convince me that I'm not worth much. Other times his tactic is the opposite: He tries to inflate my ego and make me think I'm worth more than I really am. He's crafty!

Last year I went to Russia, where I saw Satan working in a different way. There and in other Eastern-block countries, it seemed that his main way of accomplishing his purpose was through oppression and depression in the people. The people there are not tempted very much with accumulation of wealth or materialism, as we are in America. But they are very depressed.

Flying across the ocean toward home, the light turned on in my mind—I saw that Satan uses some weapons in the Soviet Union, and he uses others here. But he's working just as effectively, if not more effectively, in the United States.

Is all this talk about Satan a little depressing? That's not why I mention it. I just want to remind us all that we fight against principalities and powers. This fight against evil is a big one—in fact it's much bigger than us.

In fact, the only way to wrestle with Satan is to wrestle with God in prayer and receive God's protection. I hope you'll do that. Remember to draw near to God, and he'll draw near to you.

■ *Christian musician John Elliott has never been a wrestler, and he doesn't watch Hulk Hogan, even though he does talk about "spiritual" wrestling a lot.*

DAY 58

■ ■ ■ Not Alone

■ *Bobby Michaels*

I travel a lot. Many times, after a concert in Asia or Africa, I go back to my hotel room and feel alone.

I'm far from home, in a strange land with a different culture and customs.

Some of you have lonely times, too—most of us do. Some of us are lonely every day, others just once in a while.

To counteract those lonely times, I've learned to develop my friendship with Christ. Sound strange? I read so many passages in the Bible about Christ being our friend. (For example: "I have called you friends," in John 15:15. Also: Hebrews 13:5, Isaiah 54:10).

Sometimes I get on my knees and say, "Jesus, you promised to comfort me, and I need your presence now." Often I feel him comforting me as I pray. At other times I begin singing a song about Jesus, and as I begin to praise him I sense him drawing near to me.

Of course, sometimes I don't feel a darn thing. But in reaching out to God in faith, my attitude changes and I don't feel as lonely and as needy of companionship as I did before.

Jesus is our friend and comforter, and he wants us to reach out to him.

■ *Bobby Michaels sings in Singapore, Malaysia, China, Hong Kong, Africa, the Philippines, South Korea, and even America once in a while!*

The Convict

Randy Thomas

Back in the early 70s I was in a band called Psalm 150. One day we played at the California Men's Colony, a maximum security prison.

Our band had been on the road for days; I was tired. I played my licks that day, sang my parts, and afterwards talked to one or two prisoners. But my heart wasn't in it.

Charlie was a Christian prisoner who had helped us from the moment we got there and behaved like a true servant of Christ. Watching him, I thought about my own behavior. I thought of all the times Christ had been dead tired but still served other people.

I sat down with Charlie to ask his forgiveness for the way I had acted. Another prisoner walked by, calling Charlie "Tex" instead of Charlie. Then I looked at the lettering on his shirt—it said "Watson." Sud-denly it dawned on me: I had been talking to Tex Watson, a convicted murderer and former member of Charles Manson's gang.

"Yes, I'm guilty of the things you've heard about," he told me. "I participated in the murders. But I accepted Christ and he forgave me."

Some Christians have told me, "You can't be a Christian if you've done what Tex Watson has done." But I met the man. And I came away with a new understanding of the depths of Christ's forgiveness.

Randy Thomas of the band Allies knows God's forgiveness too.

105

DAY 60

∎∎∎ Be Yourself

∎ *Claire Cloninger*

Today people try to press everyone into molds.

We are pressured to hate the things about us that are different and to try hard to be like everyone else. But God intends each one of us to be unique and special.

Christians—of all people—ought to appreciate each other's differences and encourage each other's uniqueness.

When I was in high school, I wrote songs. But it wasn't cool then. It was embarrassing to be "arty." Once my mom wrote an article about me for the local newspaper and mentioned that I wrote songs. I was mortified. It didn't fit in with what everyone else was doing, so I didn't want anybody to know it.

Now, I've learned to view my ability to write as a precious gift of God. I'm thankful to be able to express things in music.

Encourage other people to grow and explore their uniqueness. Don't discourage or belittle the "different" skills or character traits or appearance of someone else, just because those things don't appeal to you. Just let them be themselves.

We need to learn to see others as valuable—especially the ones who are different from us.

∎ *Claire Cloninger got over her hangups about being a songwriter, and now writes tons of great songs for many Christian artists.*

106

Whither Shall We Slither?

Duffy Robbins

Recently a director was looking for talented snakes for a new movie, and a Florida man named Lou Rousso took his two-headed snake, Gertrude, to audition.

Gertrude's two heads get along fine most of the time, but at feeding time, "I have to keep them separate because the one that is not being fed will attack the one that is," says Lou. What's worse is when the two heads fight over which way to slither.

Asked in a press conference whether he thought Gertrude relay wanted to be an actress, Rousso smiled, shrugged, and said, "Well—yes and no."

Gertrude is like many of us who wonder whither we should slither. We want to do this, and we want to do that. But we can't do both at the same time, so we do nothing because we can't make up our minds.

God never said much about two-headed snakes, but he did talk about a double-minded man.

"He who doubts is like a wave on the sea, blown and tossed by the wind. That man should not think he will receive anything from the Lord; he is a double-minded man, unstable in all he does" (James 1:7–8).

God doesn't want us to be double-minded like Gertrude. He wants us to trust him, follow him, and seek him with all our hearts—without doubting.

■ *When he isn't reading funny things in the newspaper, Duffy Robbins teaches courses in youth-work at Eastern College in Pennsylvania.*

Justice on earth
■ *Michael Card*

"Here is my servant, whom I uphold, my chosen one in whom I delight. I will put my Spirit on him and he will bring justice to the nations. He will not shout or cry out or raise his voice in the streets. A bruised reed he will not break and a smoldering wick he will not snuff out. In faithfulness he will bring forth justice, he will not falter or be discouraged till he establishes justice on earth" (Isaiah 42:1–4).

When the Holy Spirit begins to delve deeply into our hearts, we begin to hunger for justice—not justice for ourselves necessarily, but justice for others, for the poor and disenfranchised to whom justice is rarely shown.

Civilization has waited thousands of years for justice to come. Occasionally it seemed to come, but in time what people thought was justice turned out to be another sort of oppression.

So we continue to look for that firm but impartial hand, for that blindfolded figure who holds the scales of justice—always finding the balance between justice and mercy. But that figure is not the bringer of justice Isaiah described.

Instead of a firm hand, Isaiah saw a manifestly gentle one—a hand that would not break a bent reed. Isaiah didn't hear the stern voice of a judge, but rather the gentle voice of someone who could barely bring himself to snuff out a candle's smoldering wick. Isaiah didn't see the blindfolded holder of the scales of justice, but rather the bearer of a cross—whose eyes were wide open.

■ ■ ■

saiah didn't see someone who served justice, but rather one who *was* Justice, and who brought justice to the nations simply by coming into the world. What Isaiah saw, of course, was the coming of Jesus of Nazareth.

So justice has come. But sadly, many of us who follow Jesus act as if we are still waiting for justice to arrive. It has been hidden in the hearts of Christ's followers all this time, and only seldom has it been glimpsed by a world hungry for justice.

If our world is to see real justice, they must see it in those who believe in Jesus. And that means the pattern which he used to reveal justice must also become our pattern, since he himself is our pattern.

Isaiah spells it out: absolute gentleness coupled with absolute faithfulness. "In faithfulness he will bring forth justice."

Micah 6:8 echoes this theme when he lists the things God requires of us: "to act justly and to love mercy and to walk humbly with your God."

Those who claim that they walk with God and that, in some sense, he walks with them, should be the bringers of justice—in gentleness, in faithfulness, and even in weakness, as Christ has shown us.

In every sphere of life—in the home as well as in the workplace, in the courts as well as in the streets—it is up to us not only to bring justice, but also in some mysterious way to *be* justice, even as he is Justice.

And by that mysterious process of dying and allowing him to live his life in us, we will bring the world justice—when we bring the world to him.

Michael Card is a Christian recording artist and Bible student.

How to live with your parents
■ *Ken Davis*

There's a basic misconception among teenagers that causes them a great deal of anxiety. That's the idea that, when their parents get up in the morning, the first thought that goes through their minds is, "How can I make them suffer today?"

My daughter probably thought that when she asked me if she could stay overnight at her friend's house. My first response was no. Maybe there was no reason to say no—it's just an automatic reflex.

But I really do love my daughter. In fact I've spent most of my life trying to save hers. When she was born the doctors struggled to save her. We brought her home and she tried to undo what they had done.

She chose to stand up for the first time at the top of the stairs going into the basement. I don't know why she chose that spot, but she did—maybe just to freak her father out. I came into the room and almost had a heart attack. I yelled her name—which scared her to death, and she fell down the stupid stairs. Fortunately, kids are made out of rubber, so she survived.

I remember when she was heading for an electrical outlet with a fork. When a child who cannot think a rational thought is crawling toward the outlet with the intent to stick a fork in there, humming, "You light up my life," the first word out of your mouth is a loud, screaming "No!"

I also remember the time I rode to the hospital with her after she had poured boiling wa-

110

ter over herself. I was praying to God, "Please allow me to take her pain." I saved her life on several occasions. That's the kind of thing that goes through my mind when she asks to sleep over at a friend's house.

If you can understand why your parents do and say the things they do, two things can happen.

First, your reaction to their saying no won't be as angry if you understand that their purpose is love, and that they are trying to protect you.

Second, you can talk to them about their decision. You may discover, for instance, that they're reluctant to let you go somewhere because they're worried about who might be driving the car. But if you reassure them that you will not ride with anyone who has been drinking or is driving carelessly, they may change their mind.

Your parents' love doesn't always look like love. If you come home late and your parents act like screaming idiots, it's not because they've been waiting up to punish you. They have been sitting up worrying about every possible horrible thing that could ever happen to you. They are so grateful to see you when you walk through the door that they threaten to kill you personally. But that's the way love acts sometimes.

How do you love your parents? You ask God to help you—it's too hard to try it on your own. And remember that loving your parents may not always change their decisions—but it will help make your home a happier, friendlier place.

Parent Ken Davis still has enough brain cells left to write books, like the one called How to Live With Your Parents Without Losing Your Mind.

Lighten up and laugh!

■ *Dan Ruple*

I've believed in laughter for years, but now all kinds of books are coming out that back up what I believe.

A lot of the books say that laughter relieves stress. One man named Norman Cousins says he was healed from cancer because he laughed. Even God agrees with me about humor. In Proverbs it says, "A joyful heart is good medicine" (17:22). Now scientists are proving that laughter releases certain chemicals in the bloodstream and nervous system that work as a relaxant.

Laughter is important for teenagers for several reasons. First, teenagers tend to be pretty self-conscious, afraid that they're uncool. But when we laugh at ourselves, we open up and relax.

Second, if you're already laughing at yourself, it won't bother you if someone else is laughing at you, too.

Laughter also helps when things get real bad. Laughing at the situation helps us to separate ourselves from it. Then we can rest and allow the Lord to take care of it.

For example, if I got up in front of my class to give an oral report and realized my zipper was down, I would be wise to be the first to laugh. That way, I'm laughing *with* everyone else.

If laughing doesn't come easy, try this: as soon as you put this book down, start smiling. Walk around that way for a while. You'll be more likely to start laughing.

Smiling, unfortunately, isn't popular today. People are always trying to look *bad*. If you

■ ■ ■

go into a hip clothing store, notice that all the models are scowling.

Fight those scowls and frowns with a smile. It'll help you to laugh, and it makes you a lot more fun to look at.

For the last eleven years I've been involved in a Christian comedy group called Isaac Air Freight. Performing in churches, we've often run into people who said, "Hey—you can't laugh in church."

That's a sad thing about Christians. Some say you have to be super-somber to be pleasing to God. Maybe they're just afraid to laugh, because my experience is the opposite: God makes me happy.

Bob Bennett and I are the cohosts of the morning talk show on a Christian radio station in California. It's a very light-hearted talk show with a very original title. We call it "Mornings with Dan and Bob." One thing we've discovered in doing that show is that people *like* humor—especially when they're driving to work in southern California traffic.

So my sermon for today is simple: Laugh at yourself. Take things easy. Lighten up and laugh!

■ *Christian deejay Dan Ruple is serious when he says laughter is important.*

Consider it done

■ Steven Curtis Chapman

Ever have a time in your Christian life when you just don't feel anything? I mean, you're saying the prayers, and going to church, and getting involved in your youth group, but nothing seems to be happening?

When I was 16 years old, a lot of people I looked up to in my church let me down. The pastor of the church, a solid Christian guy, was fired—mainly because he was preaching things we needed to hear, but some people didn't want to hear them. I was very discouraged and disillusioned. The feelings I thought should be there just weren't there anymore.

In more recent years, we've all seen some big scandals involving well-known Christians. That has discouraged many Christians (and caused many non-Christians to wonder

what kind of goofy religion we're involved in).

There are always plenty of things going on around us to take away our joy and make us feel "blah." But there's more to our faith and our relationship to God than feelings.

A lot of Christian kids are active in the youth group, go to Christian concerts, and do lots of things with Christian friends. They have plenty of good, positive emotional experiences—but they feel like God has let them down as soon as those emotions are gone.

Let's remember what God promised us—to save us and deliver us. He didn't promise to make us feel good all the time.

That's what I wanted to talk about in my song, "Consider it Done." The first few

■ ■ ■

lines of the song talk about how sometimes you want to laugh and sometimes you want to cry. We're constantly on an emotional roller coaster that seems to get bumpier the harder we try to do what God wants.

Let's face it: life is rough. And there's no way that being a Christian is going to exclude us from that. When I fail at something, when I make mistakes, I get so discouraged that I sometimes wind up spinning my wheels for a month or two. I don't know what to do.

But I need to follow the advice of Scripture and of my own song—I need to consider it done. I forget that God has already finished the work—that Jesus Christ finished the work of our salvation. When we accept that and believe it, then, like the song says, our position is to see ourselves seated with Christ, at the right hand of the Father, and to consider the work already done.

■ *Songwriter, singer, and Christian artist Steven Curtis Chapman recorded the song, "Consider it Done," on his "Real Life Conversations" album.*

■ ■ ■ Never Give Up!

■ *Guy Doud*

Winston Churchill was once asked to give a graduation speech. Churchill was a famous speaker, so everyone was waiting for a great display of oratorical skills.

But when he walked up on the stage, Churchill only said, "Young people, never give up! *Never! Never! Never!"*

It was probably the shortest graduation speech ever given, but what an important message! You should never give up on God—or on yourself.

The Bible is filled with illustrations of this, and one of my favorites is Nehemiah, who had a purpose in life—to build a wall. Others came by and mocked him. He faced conspiracy, compromise, and treachery. But Nehemiah said, "I'm doing a great work! I cannot come down!"

Our lives should be so filled with the purpose and the plan of God that like Nehemiah

we say, "I'm doing a great work! I can't come down!"

We should never give up! We need to find what purpose God has for our lives, and then put all of our talent and energy into doing it. Despite the mockery, despite the pressures of life, we can't give up.

Young people—never give up! Like Nehemiah, you're doing a great work, and you shouldn't come down for anybody!

■ *Guy Doud is a pastor and was the 1986 National Teacher of the Year.*

To Trust in God

Richie Furay

Proverbs 3 tells us: "Trust in the Lord with all your heart and lean not on your own understanding; in all your ways acknowledge him, and he will make your paths straight." Psalm 16:7 says, "I will praise the Lord, who counsels me."

To trust in God and draw counsel from him, we have to listen for God's small, still voice that gives us instruction.

Even through those dark moments when it seems nothing is ever going to work out, remember Psalm 16:8 and 9: "I have set the Lord always before me. Because he is at my right hand, I will not be shaken. Therefore my heart is glad and my tongue rejoices; my body also will rest secure."

Then, trust him—and watch him work in your life.

Let God use you in those tough situations—even when you're hurt. Let him use you to minister to people who have hurt you and dislike you. Smile at your enemies. If you can forgive them and open your heart to them, that opens the door for the Lord to really work in *your* life.

Sound unreasonable? It is. That's why we have to trust in God—not in our own understanding. I pray that your heart will be encouraged today as you watch the almighty God work in your life.

■ *Richie Furay is a Christian pastor and musician from Colorado.*

DAY 68

∎∎∎ Running

∎ *Chris Davis*

I love it when a writer can communicate in words a thought, emotion, or feeling so clearly I find myself saying, "Yes, that's exactly right."

Michel Quoist is one of those writers. This is from one of his poems:

"Lord, You have seized me and I could not resist You. I ran for a long time, but You followed me. I took bypasses, but You knew them. I struggled, You won. Here I am, Lord, out of breath, no fight left in me, and I've said yes almost unwillingly. As I stood there trembling, Your look of love fell on me."

Because I ran from God for a long time myself, I read this poem over and over. The Holy Spirit really does seize us as we're running and hiding and prolonging our own agony. We all have that God-shaped vacuum in us that only the Lord can fill.

Has the Holy Spirit been tugging on your sleeve—or your heart—lately?

I invite you today to stop running and give your heart totally to God. Read these passages if you want some help: Philippians 3:7–8 and verse 12. But please don't try to run from your loving Father any more.

∎ *Chris Davis is still running, but it's not from the Lord. It's all over the world to play concerts with the band Glad.*

Not Without a Doubt

Solveig Leithaug

I'm in my early twenties now, but when I was between fourteen and seventeen, doubt was a big problem in my life. Sometimes I didn't feel anything to indicate God was there.

Many young people struggle with doubt every day: "How do I know if Jesus is there?" "How do I know I'm a Christian?"

If you have doubts, just remember that you aren't alone. Most Christians struggle with doubt, even Christian leaders. The Bible is full of doubters. Peter denied Christ three times, and Thomas wouldn't believe Christ had risen from the dead until he put his hands in Jesus' wounds.

I am still attacked by doubt, but I've found a way to deal with it. I talk to Jesus—even when I'm not one hundred percent convinced he's hearing me—and I say, "I don't really know if you're here right now, but I come to you with the little faith that I have. Please make my faith stronger."

We need to admit to our doubts, rather than hide them. Too many people wear a mask that says, "I am holy and perfect. I have no problems—everything is wonderful." Don't hide behind a mask. Share your doubts with God and other Christians.

And don't be upset by doubt. The fact that you're asking questions shows that you're trying to be honest about what you believe.

 Solveig Leithaug lives in Norway, but travels to America to sing and record.

119

God has great plans for you

■ *Phil Madeira*

A few years ago my mom sent me some Bible verses, which I read once, put on my refrigerator, and quickly forgot about. About a month later, a friend sent me the same verses. I thought maybe somebody was trying to tell me something, so I memorized them.

The verses are found in Jeremiah 29:11–13: " 'For I know the plans I have for you,' declares the Lord, 'plans to prosper you and not to harm you, plans to give you hope and a future. Then you will call upon me and come and pray to me, and I will listen to you. You will seek me and find me when you seek me with all your heart.' "

These are important verses, because many of us start the day thinking that our lives are going nowhere. Maybe the circumstances in our lives are so bad that we can't even imagine that God has something wonderful for us.

My life revolves around a dream—the dream of performing music and making records that glorify God. Often, as I've pursued that dream, I've wondered whether God or anybody else cares about me. I've questioned my own worthiness to fulfill that dream.

Don't we all feel that way? We feel like the little guy who's not noticed by God or the world, helpless.

W hat's your dream? Do you have one? And if you do, do you ever find yourself wondering whether you're ever going to achieve it? Does God care? Is he helping you?

These verses tell us that God has plans for us. Let that

■ ■ ■

sink in. Many of us focus on the don'ts, the do's and all the rules we try to follow to make sure God likes us. But these verses tell us, "Hey, I want to prosper you." Just like a good earthly father who wants to see his kids succeed, God's plan is to prosper us. He's got a plan, a hope, and a future for us— including a nice place in heaven, as well as a positive future in this life. But he does require something of us: that we come to him, pray to him, and seek his will. Then he promises to listen to us and bless us.

But the best part of this passage is at the end. It says we will find God when we seek him with our whole hearts.

So many of us go half-heartedly after God. We want the gold (whether it's gold records or the kind of gold you can spend) and the easy life and all the goodies God has for us. But he tells us: "Seek me with your whole heart. Get to know me. It's a great life I'm offering you."

God has great plans for you. Seek him, and his will, with your whole heart.

■ *Phil Madeira doesn't have that gold record yet, but he has made a few records that everyone agrees are great.*

A God's-eye view of ourselves

■ *Pete Carlson*

One of the biggest issues in our lives is our self-concept, or how we view ourselves.

Our self-concept also affects the people close to us, and how we relate to them, love them, and care for them. It's hard to reach out and love other people when we don't understand or love ourselves.

Where does this self-concept problem come from? It first appears during our early childhood. When you're young, you want to look cute and good all the time. Most kids want approval and a sense of belonging.

Small children always want someone to see what they're doing. It's not enough just to do it—you've got to have an audience, too.

Remember the first time you dove off the high diving board at the swimming pool? Going off that high dive for the very first time is pretty scary in itself. But we will kill ourselves to get our parents to pay attention and watch us do it. It's not enough to just jump off—we want them to see us, and approve.

There's nothing wrong with children wanting attention. There *is* a problem if we don't control that tendency as we grow older. Does anyone at your school still suck his thumb? If so, you probably think he's a bit strange. Our need for approval is the same way; it's perfectly normal when you're a toddler, but as you grow older you need to put it behind you. Accept yourself—don't spend your life seeking approval and attention.

■ ■ ■

As we get older, some of us start getting our sense of self-worth by accumulating things. We gather these around us until we can point to our pile of possessions and say, "Hey—this is me. Ain't I great?"

But that isn't the way Christians are to act. Jesus tells us that we are made in his image. We are important and valuable to him—not because of all the things, friends or status we accumulate, but because he created us and loved us enough to die for us.

I pray for us all that we will begin to see our value—to see ourselves not as an accumulation of things, or our jobs, or who we know, but as God sees us: as individuals created in his image who are valuable to him just as we are.

■ *Pete Carlson is a Nashville-based singer and songwriter whose songs probably appear on some albums you own.*

■ ■ ■ Becoming Wise

■ *Al Menconi*

How can we become wise? The Bible tells us in Proverbs 1:7. The first step is to trust and reverence the Lord. Easy to say—but do we really? What is trust, anyway?

Here's a good way to understand and remember what *trust* is:

T is for Totally
R is for Rely
U is for Upon
S is for Simple
T is for Truth.

So trust means we must *totally rely upon simple truth* of God's word.

Once a man was trying to get across a pond covered with thin ice. He knew he couldn't walk or jump on the ice, so he had to lie down on the ice and inch his way across by spreading out his weight. That's exactly what the Bible's Greek word for trust means: to be totally stretched out upon. And that's how we should trust God. We can't have one foot on one side and one foot on the other side. We must fully rely on God's simple truths.

■ *Al Menconi is head honcho at Menconi ministries.*

Facing Up to Sin

Rich Mullins

If I had two minutes to share something urgent with you today, I would say this:

The most important thing you need to know about God is that he is holy and that he is unapproachable. He's unapproachable only because we're sinful. And if you want to know God, you have to have your sins taken away.

Sin is not a popular topic today. It's not much fun acknowledging that we've blown it in God's sight. And many people today don't give much credit to the idea of sin.

But sin is like a lot of other things in the Christian walk: If you want to know God, you have to do it on his terms.

God says that he is holy and we are sinful. And we'll just have to accept that, be-cause you ain't gonna change his mind about it. Acknowledge that you are sinful, that he is holy, and that life comes from him—because we will only experience life to the degree that we understand and know him.

Sin isn't the end of the road for us. It's the beginning. In fact, the only way to really know God, the only way to come into his presence, is through Christ. If our sin forces us to realize that we can't clean up our own act and that we need Christ, then that's good.

Rich Mullins is a Nash-ville-based singer, song-writer, and sinner.

Putting ourselves on the line

■ *Scott Wesley Brown*

The first time I was in the Soviet Union, I was invited to sing in a Russian church service.

I was totally nervous—I figured the moment I stood up to sing, Soviet soldiers or KGB agents would rush the stage and haul me off to Siberia and I'd never be heard from again. I sat at the pulpit with the pastor, my knees knocking together. In fact, I was thinking of telling the pastor I didn't feel well and shouldn't sing.

At that point, he leaned toward me and said, "Brother, please be careful of the words you speak tonight, because there are certain government officials in the congregation." Thanks, Pal! That's just what I needed to get my confidence up!

Then another thought came to my mind. I thought of the incredible freedom we have in America. We don't have to worry about what we say; we can preach freely and proclaim the gospel in our schools, at our jobs, in our homes, and in our neighborhoods. God has given us so much, and he has equipped us so greatly to share the gospel of Jesus Christ.

I thought how frightening it must be for these Russian people. Every day, they have to fight the fear of being cut down by the KGB, which monitors their activities and questions their service to the Lord.

I turned to the pastor and said, "Doesn't all this frighten you?" I'll never forget his answer. He leaned toward me and said in his strong Russian accent, "Brother, we are on the winning team!"

That blew me away. We are on the winning team, and there is no KGB or any power that can come against us when we take that bold radical stand for Jesus.

And if these brothers can do it in Russia, where there is the reality of prison camp or torture, then certainly we who live in a free society should stand that much more boldly for Jesus in our country.

But it isn't that easy, is it? The fear that I experienced in Russia was the same fear that I felt in high school, walking down the hallways thinking something could happen to me if I tell my friends about Jesus. Sure, they won't put me in prison or torture me, but they might reject me or make fun of me for being a Christian.

I'm still learning that we are on the winning team. Even if we suffer imprisonment or rejection, God will honor our stand for him.

We all have to be willing to take that kind of a risk, because when we gave our life to Christ, we entered his service. We need to follow his orders—regardless of the risk. It might mean death and imprisonment. Or it might be rejection or embarrassment at school.

The Word of God says that we have to deny ourselves and pick up our cross and follow him. Our Christian brothers and sisters in Russia are doing this at great cost. Can we follow their example in school?

Christian artist and singer Scott Wesley Brown regularly visits behind the Iron Curtain with his organization, I Care.

You are what you think

■ *Bill Walden*

I've been a committed Christian for six years, but for seven years before that I was a backslidden Christian. I did a lot of damage to myself during that time, and part of that damage still haunts me because, every day, Satan brings sinful thoughts to my mind.

Sometimes it seems like Satan can put whatever he wants into my mind, and I can't resist those thoughts. But that's not true. I've been learning to control my own mind.

We all have choices everyday about what things we will think about. Some things will lead us closer to God, while others will lead us farther away. Even if bad thoughts come to our mind, it's our decision to choose what we will do about them.

God tells us that what oc-cupies our mind is really important to him. And he gives us some guidelines about the kinds of things he wants us to concentrate on:

"Finally, brothers, whatever is true, whatever is noble, whatever is right, whatever is pure, whatever is lovely, whatever is admirable—if anything is excellent or praisesworthy—think about such things" (Philippians 4:8).

Thinking is a bit like physical exercise. It may not be fun to get up in the morning and run three miles, but we know it helps the body. We can condition our mind the same way by exercising our brain to think about good things.

But there will still be times when doubts, temptations, lust, anger, or other thoughts crowd into our minds. Here are some

of the things I do to fight off these mental attacks.

One is to resist Satan by standing firm on God's Word. I do this by remembering the times that God has been faithful to me and the times his Word has come true for me as I trusted him. I have six years worth of positive experiences with God, and I think about them.

Another is to realize that I am weak and have sinned before. So when I find myself in a situation where temptation is strong, I run in the opposite direction. I don't give myself a chance to yield to temptation.

When I am attacked by an evil thought, I speak against it in the name of the Lord. I don't want to get over-spiritual here, but I just say: "Wait, this thought is not of God. Leave me alone, Satan. Get out of my face. Don't harass me now."

God will protect us from evil if we let him.

Another way is to address the issue before it comes up. For me, that means being with God daily in prayer and Bible reading. In Psalm 119, David says, "I have hidden your words in my heart." This is our spiritual defense system.

The mind is a wonderful thing, capable of great beauty or great evil. By focusing our minds on God and good things, we can fight off evil thoughts and head off temptation before it traps us.

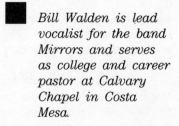

Bill Walden is lead vocalist for the band Mirrors and serves as college and career pastor at Calvary Chapel in Costa Mesa.

Focusing on the big picture

■ *Randy Stonehill*

Here's a shocking revelation: we all have problems! Since we know that, the next step—and the most important one for us as Christians— is deciding what we will do about our problems.

Unfortunately, many of us do the wrong thing when times get tough. We cop out. We become escapists. We take our troubles as an excuse for sin, and we use flaky excuses like: "I don't feel so good. I need to go blow off some steam." We compound our problems and distance ourselves from God and actually postpone finding the solution.

It's when things are really tough and painful that we have to raise our sights above the seemingly impenetrable wall of our immediate needs. We need to get God's perspective on our lives and our problems, and be true to our calling even though it doesn't seem fun at the moment.

Here's a passage that has helped me during these times:

"Therefore, since we have been justified through faith, we have peace with God through our Lord Jesus Christ, through whom we have gained access by faith into this grace in which we now stand. And we rejoice in the hope of the glory of God" (Romans 5:1–2).

That passage and many others remind me that I am justified and have peace with God now, no matter how stormy the seas around my little boat may look. Passages like this have helped me focus on the big picture when things are going bad and when temptations

and tough hurdles come my way.

The Bible is the Sword of the Word. I'm afraid we've heard that so many times we don't hear it anymore. The Bible has been an immeasurable help to me. After all, God knows what he's talking about and it's all in there.

Sometimes it washes over me like a healing tide, and I say, "Oh yeah, this is it!" It brings me back into focus. Other times I don't feel anything, but I'm hiding the Word in my heart. Over time it makes a difference. Try it, and you'll be surprised how it crops up as a really useful weapon when you need it the most.

Another thing that is a great comfort is talking to God as my Father. Telling my problems, fears, and troubles to the Lord helps me get a better handle on things. Fears are real scary when they're in the dark

going "Booga! Booga!" But when I pull them out and talk to God I see things for what they are. Then problems aren't big scary monsters; they're more like little grease smudges in my life.

When we act out our faith in obedience and choose to trust the Lord—even when it goes against what we're feeling or what our intellect tells us—our hope in sharing God's glory is reinforced. It's here that we get to see the hand of God at work in our little lives.

When you realize God is watching and caring for you, then your problems begin to take on their proper perspective in the big picture.

 Randy Stonehill has tackled a lot of big, scary problems in his ten albums.

Wearing our colors for Christ

■ *Rick Cua*

When I first came to the Lord I was like a chameleon—you know, the little lizard that changes colors whenever it finds itself in a new situation.

Sure, I loved the Lord. But in church I was one way, and then out there on the streets with my friends who didn't know the Lord, I was another way.

I was going along with the crowd a little too often. I wasn't sharing the Lord with people, and if I was in a circle of friends that were telling bad jokes, I would grin and chuckle along with them—just trying to fit in.

But one day something happened that hit me like a brick. I was reading the Bible and came across Mark 8:38, where Jesus says: "If anyone is ashamed of me and my words in this adulterous and sinful generation, the Son of Man will be ashamed of him when he comes in his Father's glory with the holy angels."

I realized something horrible: I was ashamed of Jesus Christ. I was bowled over, because I realized that this verse meant what it said. I was ashamed to be a follower of Christ's, which meant that, when Jesus returns, he would be ashamed of me.

I confessed my weakness to the Lord; since then, he has helped me to stand up boldly for him.

Years later, my wife Diana and I were watching some motorcycle guys who were wearing their jackets, which they call their "colors." And we thought about high-school teams and pro teams wearing the jackets with

their colors. We realized that everybody has their colors, and Diana thought up the idea for the song, "Wear Your Colors."

What we're saying in that song is that, as Christians, we ought to wear our colors for Christ—not physical colors like red, yellow, or blue, but the colors of our belief and our way of life.

That means being a Christian around the clock—not just when it's easy, like at a Christian concert, in your youth group, at church, or with your Christian friends. I'm talking about when you go to work or school with people who aren't saved.

That's when you need to lift that banner of Jesus higher. If there's some funky talk going on, you need to walk away. If people are doing something that's not right, you need to tell them, "I can't do this."

I'm not saying you need to be like a bull in a china shop, or pull out your Bible and start yelling, screaming, jumping on the table, and preaching to them. The point is that our actions can sometimes speak louder than words. If something funky's going on, just leave. They'll know something's wrong. There'll be a chill in that room.

Sure, people will make fun of you. It might make you feel bad. But those same people will want to get next to you when they realize you've got a lot more guts than they do. And Jesus will want to get next to you too—if you're not ashamed to wear his colors!

The song, "Wear Your Colors," is from Rick's album of the same name.

■ ■ ■ Take Heart!

■ *Billy Sprague*

Disappointment and discouragement are realities, but so is the power of Christ's love to take care of our hurt.

That's why Wayne Kirkpatrick wrote "A Heart Like Mine," and that's why I recorded it.

We all face disappointment and discouragement, whether it's a lost spelling bee, the time you didn't make the team, a letter of rejection from a college, a broken relationship, a miscarriage, or whatever.

Disappointment is real. Jesus knew that. He said, "In this world you *will* have trouble. But take heart! I have overcome the world" (John 16:33).

So what do I do when I feel overcome by the world? I hurt. And I cry out to the Lord for relief just like David did in the Psalms. The Psalms really show us how emotionally real David was with his disappointments and heartaches. And they show us that God really does have good things in mind for us (see Jeremiah 29:11).

We aren't exempt from disappointment and shattered dreams, but we do have someone to comfort and heal us so that we can go on with hope. When you doubt that, look up these verses: 1 Peter 5:7; 2 Corinthians 1:3, 4; Revelation 7:17; and Isaiah 25:8.

■ *Billy Sprague is a youthworker, musician, and recording artist.*

God's Answer

Roger Judd

Roger Judd is a graphic artist and free-lance car-toonist living in Upland, Indiana, with his wife and daughter.

Loving the unlovely

■ Guy Doud

I was in college. It was finals week, and I was really bummed out. I'd felt pretty secure in college, but soon I'd be leaving that security to go out into the world, look for a job, find a home, live by myself, and make money.

The thought was frightening, so I went downtown to a restaurant and ordered a big breakfast. In those days, that's what I did to escape from my problems or to treat myself— ate a lot.

As I sat there eating and looking out the window, down the street came the two ugliest people I had ever seen. The man had a huge cauliflower ear, and the woman had warts all over her face with hairs growing out of them.

I thought, *How disgusting!* I waited for them to pass by because looking at them made me feel uncomfortable.

But they didn't pass by. They came into the restaurant and sat down at the counter. They were poorly dressed and poorly groomed, and as I sat there watching them I lost my appetite.

And then a mother with a blonde-haired, beautiful little girl with big blue eyes came into the restaurant.

The two ugly people sitting at the counter said, "Oh, look at that pretty little girl!" That grotesque-looking man got a nickel out of his coin purse and said, "Come here, sweetie. I want to give you a kiss."

I was about ready to jump out of my seat. I wanted to say, "How dare you, you ugly, grotesque thing, ask that beautiful, blonde-headed, blue-eyed,

clean, well-dressed little girl to give *you* a kiss!"

The girl looked up at her mother with questioning eyes, and the mother looked back as if to say, "It's up to you, honey." And the little girl walked up to the man and she placed one hand on one cheek and one hand on the other, and she brought her face up to his face and she kissed him. And I saw a change come over that man. Then the little girl went over to the lady sitting at the counter and gave her a hug.

That morning was worth a month of sermons on what it means to be accepted by Christ in our ugliness—the ugliness of our sin.

I was reminded of a poster that my roommate had up in our room at college. It had a picture of a drunk in the gutter, with an empty bottle beside him. The caption read: "You only love Jesus Christ as much as the person you love least."

That little girl showed me what Jesus meant when he said "Whatever you did for one of the least of these brothers of mine, you did for me" (Matt. 26:40).

We only love Jesus as much as the ones we love least. That's taken on a totally different significance for me now. In God's sight sin has made us ugly, but in Jesus' eyes, we can all be made whole and clean.

Guy Doud is a pastor, school teacher, and public speaker.

Amazing grace

■ *Steven Curtis Chapman*

God loves us and cares for us infinitely, but that doesn't mean he's giving us a blank check for us to do whatever we want.

Instead, he tells us, "Be holy even as I am holy." That can be pretty frustrating—until you realize that we can only be holy through Jesus Christ.

My pastor said it well: "Every time we read that Scripture, we see God's expectations of what we're supposed to be growing farther and farther ahead of us." And it's true. We see ourselves miles behind where we should be, trying to catch up.

We may take a few steps forward, and it looks like God's goals are just about within our reach—and then we are taught by the Holy Spirit about a certain problem in our lives, and God's expectations seem way out there far in front of us again. But that difference between where we are and where we're supposed to be is where the grace of Jesus Christ covers us.

Grace is a powerful concept, and it's a powerful source of help and comfort in our Christian lives. I tried to explore it in the song called "Tuesday's Child," which is based on the old Mother Goose rhyme: "Tuesday's child is full of grace."

Christ has covered us with grace. To me, that means that when God looks at us he doesn't see our sin and failings, but Christ's grace. When the father sees us, it's through the blood of Christ.

Understanding grace helps us understand some other pas-

■ ■ ■

sages in the Bible. The Scriptures tell us that God hears the prayers of a righteous man. But who's righteous? *I* certainly don't feel righteous. But God *sees* us as righteous because of the work of Jesus Christ.

Pray that the Holy Spirit will make grace real to you. Open the Bible and see for yourself—don't take my word for it.

As we come to understand more about God's magnificent grace, we will start to see what our place is in Christ, and how his grace has covered us. Then we can begin to see ourselves the same way the Father sees us.

The eternal work of God's grace in your life was finished on the cross, but it will never be completed in our lives. We need to appropriate that grace and apply it in our lives every day. That's a real challenge to

us, especially to young people. But I believe that youth are the ones who are really affecting the world for Jesus Christ. At a conference called D.C. '88, I saw 8,000 committed kids with a radical, genuine desire to go out and touch their world for Jesus.

We can only do that if we see where we are in Jesus Christ and that his grace has covered us. That's what gives us the strength to tell people that Jesus is the answer for their lives.

■ *Steven Curtis Chapman recorded the song "Tuesday's Child" for his second Sparrow album, "Real Life Conversations."*

Beat the habit

■ *Tom Beard*

Just when you thought it was safe to go back in the water, it surfaces again. Like a big underwater shark, that old dorsal fin is heading straight for you. That habit that you know is sinful and breaks God's heart (you know, the one you thought you blew out of the water at church last Sunday) is coming to claim you as a victim—again.

It's time to kill the monster once and for all. Here's how.

Step One. *Burn Romans 6:6–9 into your soul.* This passage tells you that your old sinful nature has been nailed to a cross with Jesus. It's dead. You can put it away.

Step Two. *Picture yourself dead to sin.* Sin is a real, active force. Satan is stomping around, making noise and wanting to swallow you whole (1 Peter 5:8).

So, to get rid of sin's effect on your life, you've got to kill it as Christ has killed it through his death. Talk to your mirror. Tell the image you see that you've died to sin and that Christ lives in you.

Step Three. *Compare the law of gravity to the law of sin.* What goes up, must come down. It's simple.

Sin is the same way. What results from sin is death. Nothing but death. It will help to realize you're a slave no matter what, but you have a choice as to who you're going to be a slave to (Romans 6:20–23).

Step Four. *Personalize Romans 6:6–9.* This brings us back to step one, but with a twist. Whenever you see "our" or "we," replace it with your

name in the proper context. Once a day isn't too often for this step.

Step Five. *Don't give any room to your flesh.* Romans 8 has so much to say about life in the spirit versus life in the flesh. Your spirit is new (2 Corinthians 5:17). You are dead to sin, so there's no room for your flesh to rule you. Put it down.

Step Six. *Be accountable to yourself and God every day (1 Peter 4:1–6).* Don't let a day go by without a time of prayer during which you rejoice with God over your victories in certain areas. Or if you've blown it and sinned, hurting as God hurts, confessing your sins and accepting his forgiveness.

Accountability is vital. You need an outside force to spur you on. You may need to choose to ask a Christian brother or sister to pray with you about your habit and to hold you accountable to them. See if that doesn't motivate you to do something about it (Hebrews 3:13)!

Step Seven. *Yield your body to God (Romans 6:19–23).* It's his. He bought it, paid for it, saved it, washed it, and loves it. Now it's time for you to love it too.

Not only should you love your body, but you should use your body to love God. And if you love him, to keep his commandments (1 John 5:3–5).

Sure, it's tough. But God promises eternal life to those who beat sin. And we have everything we need to do it (1 Peter 1:3–4). So go for it!

Tom Beard, a former member of the Christian band Glad, is now a popular solo performer.

The storm—or the boat?

■ *Dana Key*

Eddie DeGarmo and I have often taken some criticism for the type of music we play. But at one point several years ago, we'd heard all of the criticism and derision and seen all of the angry, pointed fingers we could stand. We gave up in frustration and discouragement and laid down our music.

We both got jobs, and everything seemed to be going along fine—at least externally. But we weren't at peace with ourselves or with God.

Then a friend named David came to see me. He began talking about the time Christ came to his disciples walking on the water (Matthew 14:22–23). All of the disciples stayed in the boat except for Peter.

"Most people think the point of the story is that Peter didn't have enough faith to walk on the water with Christ—that he failed, and Christ had to reach out his hand and save him." David shook his head. "They're missing it. The point of the story is that Peter was the only one with enough faith to join Jesus in the midst of the storm, while the others were enjoying their safe, dry seats in the boat."

Then David leaned forward and looked right into my eyes. "Dana," he said, "you're one of those disciples still enjoying a safe, secure seat in the boat while Jesus is calling you out into the storm."

This doesn't happen to me very often, but as soon as David said that, I recognized the voice of my Savior. I realized at that moment what I've seen

■ ■ ■

proven many times since—that it's far better to be in the storm where Jesus is than in a dry, safe boat alone.

What is God calling you to do right now? Has he given you love for someone in trouble? Has he put it on your heart to reach out to others in sacrificial, liberating love? Maybe God has shown you people around you who are hurting and lonely and who need you to show them God's love. Maybe God wants you to begin to show some leadership for Christ at school or church, to step out of your comfort zone and to take some risks.

Whatever God is calling you to do, the first step in learning what it is and tackling it is turning your life over to him.

Take a moment and whisper this prayer:

Dear Jesus, thank you for dying for me, and please give me the power to live for you. Lord, please use me anywhere and in any way you desire as I offer to you everything I am and everything I hope to become.

God bless you as you seek to be a channel of God's liberating love.

 This discussion was taken from Dana's brand-new book about Christian music, Don't Stop the Music *(Zondervan, 1989).*

■ ■ ■ What's Joy?

■ *Mike Warnke*

It takes strength to be a Christian. So where can we get that strength?

The source of all our strength is joy. And joy comes from our love for God (like the Bible says: "The joy of the Lord is our strength").

Some people wonder what joy is. Is it always being happy? Is it being giddy and dancing and singing and laughing?

Nope. Joy means being able to believe in a mountaintop when you're in the deepest pit that you've ever been in. Joy means believing in the light when you're in the deepest darkness you've ever been in. Joy means being able to feel the hand of God on your shoulder when you're confused and frightened—and it doesn't seem like God is around. Joy is a gift from God.

Joy is one thing Satan can't rob us of—we can only give it up. None of us need to do that, but if we do here's how to get the joy back.

The best way is to refresh your memory and renew your mind about what the promises of God are. You can do this by getting into his Word—regularly, faithfully.

Remember God's promise to you: "The one who is in you is greater than the one who is in the world" (I John 4:4). Focus on that promise, and God's other promises, regardless of your circumstances. That's the way to get your joy back!

■ *Christian speaker Mike Warnke mixes humor with teaching for joyful results.*

Who's the Fool?

Al Menconi

The book of Proverbs tells us to be on the lookout for fools. Here are ten ways to recognize one, along with Scripture references from Proverbs so you can look them up yourself.

1) A fool doesn't obey his parents (1:7–8 and 11:29).

2) A fool won't take advice (12:15 and 26:7).

3) A fool is lazy (6:6–11 and 12:11).

4) A fool is a liar and a troublemaker (6:12–15 and 10:23).

5) A fool seeks company with those who will entice him to do wrong (6:32, all of chapter 7, and 15:14).

6) A fool is a bigmouth who can't control his tongue (17:27–28 and 18:2, 6, 7).

7) A fool is a hothead (20:3, 29:8, and 29:20–22).

8) A fool doesn't think ahead (13:16, 15:28, and 22:3).

9) A fool is easily bored (14:14).

10) A fool eats and drinks improperly (13:25, 20:1, and 23:29–35).

Being a fool is pretty bad, but there is one thing worse—a man who is "wise in his own eyes" (Proverbs 26:12). When you say, "I don't act like a fool," you might have more trouble with your pride.

■ *We know Al Menconi, and he's no fool.*

True friendship
■ *Richie Furay*

Has someone hurt you lately? Or taken advantage of you? Maybe someone said something that was cruel, or just unloving, or maybe untrue.

Now, walking around the halls at school, you try to avoid them. It's uncomfortable. You ask yourself, *How could this happen?*

I've been in situations like this, too, and I've found that it's helpful to remember what Jesus said: "Do not let your hearts be troubled. Trust in God; trust also in me" (John 14:1).

God is building Christian character in your life. He's building the fruit of the Spirit in you (you can look that up in Galatians 5:22–23). He's asking you to draw near to him as James says in his epistle (4:8). And he promises to stick with you like

no other friend can. As he told Joshua, "I will never leave you or fail you."

It may even be your faith that caused people to hurt you. Maybe deep down inside, they want to be like you, to be able to make the stand that you've made, but they just don't have the courage.

Right now, whether you're hurting or not, the Lord wants you to let him live through you. He wants to touch you. He wants you to be more and more aware of his presence in your life. He wants to be more real to you, as you learn to trust him.

Right now, while you're hurting, there's no friend better for you than Jesus. He knows exactly what you're going through—the rejection, the lone-

■ ■ ■

liness, the misunderstanding, the cruel words.

When I'm hurting, I think of Jesus' trial and death (look in Isaiah 53 and the Gospels). He said, "Father, forgive them, for they do not know what they are doing." He was concerned about others more than himself.

Jesus is our high priest who has been touched with the feelings of our infirmities. In all ways he has been tempted even as we are. So Jesus knows—he knows the hurt and the pain and the sorrow that's gripping your heart right now. He knows better than anyone.

He knows your need. And if you look to him, he will strengthen you (Philippians 4:13). He will get you through the situation.

What a joy to know that he's our friend!

■ *Richie Furay, a former member of the bands Buffalo Springfield and Poco, now pastors a church in Boulder, Colorado.*

■ ■ ■ God's Hand

■ Billy Sprague

In 1981 and 1982 I went through months of depression because of a broken relationship.

This wasn't the mild melancholy that hits all of us from time to time; this depression hurt. I walked around in a haze; I couldn't eat; I couldn't sleep.

For the first time in my life, I understood the deep, numbing pain that drives people to suicide. And it was only the Lord's invisible hand that brought me through.

It helped to realize that I wasn't the first person in the world to feel like this. Psalm 102 says: "For my days vanish like smoke; my bones burn like glowing embers. My heart is blighted and withered like grass; I forget to eat my food. . . . I lie awake; I have become like a bird alone on a roof" (verses 3, 4, and 7).

And it helped to know that God was with me (even though it didn't feel like it), and that he shared my pain. Over a period of time, that helped bring me out of it.

Then, with Jim Weber's help, I wrote a song to those who are "walking so close to the edge" and feeling like I'd felt. The main message of the song is: "Jesus is the love strong enough to keep you, and he won't let you go."

Remember that when you're walking close to the edge.

■ *Christian artist Billy Sprague is feeling better now, thank you.*

148

Forgetting Yourself

Rich Mullins

Christianity isn't about being self-*sacrificing*—it's about being self-*forgetting*. Forget yourself once in a while, and open your eyes.

Focus on this big, beautiful world God has made. If you walk to school, learn to identify every plant that you pass on the way. At night, learn to identify every constellation in the sky. Get to know birds by their feathers, flight patterns, and songs.

It's a big world—and it reflects the character of God.

People who become self-centered lose contact with the outside world. They spend all their time and energy worrying about bad grades, or unfriendly friends, or mean parents. Forget about those things once in a while, and allow yourself to become involved in the lives of people who have equally bad situations. Open up and let other people matter to you.

When we take a bigger view of things, God will give us more grace and love for others. We'll find ourselves responding to the needs and to the goodness; we'll find ourselves angered by injustice to others.

And we'll have a bigger appreciation of even small things, like the smell of a wet dog on a mucky day. Let go of yourself—and God will show you a whole new world.

■ *For more from Rich Mullins on this big, big world and our big, big God, listen to his songs "Verge of a Miracle" or "Awesome God."*

■ ■ ■ Thanking God

■ *Claire Cloninger*

It was a cool fall day. I was sitting quietly on our back deck looking at the beautiful things—the potted plants with their bright colors, the red-winged blackbirds.

I found myself thanking God for the wonderful job he had done. At first, I felt silly. I was talking to God like he was a second grader who had brought me a good spelling paper. But praise *is* something like that—we turn toward God and express our appreciation for who he is and what he's done.

But it's hard to praise God when we're unhappy about something. When we dislike ourselves or our bodies, it's like saying, "You didn't use good taste when you made me." But God used his wisdom when he made everything—even me and you.

When we thank God for everything he gives us, it's a way to line our hearts up with him. God built this whole world around us so that we could enjoy it. It must break his heart when we don't even notice or thank him for what he's done for us.

Even if you don't have a backyard like mine, find a place today where you can quiet your heart and mind and stop and thank God for all he has given you.

■ *Claire Cloninger has written a book about looking at God's world. It's called "The Kaleidoscope."*

The Simplicity of Christ

Ian Tanner

I was raised in a religious home. I wasn't a Christian, but I was very interested in religion. My friend and I used to read about different religions and argue about them endlessly.

But then my friend became a Christian, and he told me, "Ian, God isn't complex. It's very simple. You need to be born again."

I was like many people—I had my doubts about a lot of Christians. But somehow, my friend touched me. He wasn't sinless; in fact, he still struggled with partying and other things we enjoyed at school. But I saw God changing him. I didn't have to believe his words, I could see the change happening in him before my eyes.

Everybody is looking for God, one way or another. Today, people find New Age religions attractive. I understand that—I used to be fascinated with religious things, too. But even though it's interesting, it's junk. It's not real.

People are looking for God within themselves—but God isn't inside us. He's outside, waiting to come in. For me, accepting Christ and his control of my life wasn't easy. It took time to put away partying and other sins. But God changed my attitude and my behavior. Nobody could have argued me into becoming a Christian, but when I saw what Christ had done to my friend, all my complicated arguments evaporated.

■ *When Ian Tanner isn't playing with his band The Awakening, he works in The Carpenter's Shop bookstore in Stratford, Ontario.*